CRYSTAL PRESCRIPTIONS

Volume 8

Crystals for Prosperity
The A-Z Guide

CRYSTAL
PRESCRIPTIONS
Volume 8

Crystals for Prosperity
The A-Z Guide

Judy Hall

Author of the best-selling

The Crystal Bible series

Winchester, UK
Washington, USA

JOHN HUNT PUBLISHING

First published by O-Books, 2020
O-Books is an imprint of John Hunt Publishing Ltd., 3 East St., Alresford,
Hampshire SO24 9EE, UK
office@jhpbooks.com
www.johnhuntpublishing.com
www.o-books.com

For distributor details and how to order please visit the 'Ordering' section on
our website.

ISBN: 978 1 78904 240 5
978 1 78904 241 2 (ebook)
Library of Congress Control Number: 2018961972

A CIP catalogue record for this book is available from the British Library.

Design: Stuart Davies

UK: Printed and bound by CPI Group (UK) Ltd, Croydon, CR0 4YY
Printed in North America by CPI GPS partners

Disclaimer

The crystals, rituals and layouts in this book do not constitute financial advice nor
do they guarantee rapid success. Your prosperity depends on how well aligned your
inner and outer intentions are and how positively focused you remain and only you
can achieve this. Nevertheless it is sincerely hoped that the book contributes to
your becoming enriched in every way.

We operate a distinctive and ethical publishing philosophy
in all areas of our business, from our global network of
authors to production and worldwide distribution.

Contents

Volumes in this series

About the Author

Judy Hall is an internationally-known crystal facilitator and author. Her *Crystal Bibles* are the best-selling crystal books in the US, UK and elsewhere. Judy runs workshops for all levels of experience. Fascinated with crystals and stones since she was a child, Judy remembers using crystals to heal and generate energy in her previous lives: a skill that she has instinctively drawn on in her present life. Her lifelong interest in the history of stones and curiosity as to how their properties were first identified has been satisfied by studying for a Master's Degree in Cultural Astronomy and Astrology in which she examined connections between the sky, gods, planets, stones and healing practices across many ancient cultures. Judy has been using crystals in her healing and astrological work for almost fifty years and created the exercises in this book to ensure her own crystal prosperity and that of her clients.

Introduction: What is prosperity?

Prosperity is a way of living and thinking, and not just money or things. Poverty is a way of living and thinking, and not just a lack of money or things.
Eric Butterworth

Crystals have been used for thousands of years as a means to attract abundance. This book shares how you too can create crystal prosperity for yourself. It looks at what prosperity is and how to attract abundance of all kinds into your life with the assistance of appropriate crystals. I know from a lifetime working with crystals that they amplify, potentise and manifest our deepest desires and act as powerful attractors. You'll discover what works best for you and how you are going to interact with the magic of crystals. This is a richness you then take into any area of your life.

There have been many pathways mapped out to abundance in recent years. You may have tried the manifestation process and perhaps it hasn't worked. You've put in your cosmic order, tried to uncover The Secret, followed The Law of Attraction and, so far as you can see, your deepest desire hasn't yet manifested. Or has it and you simply haven't realised what that deepest desire actually was? Continual blocking may be a sign that there is something fundamentally confused or unwise about what you seek. It may be that there are core beliefs, toxic thoughts, karmic debts or soul intentions that are not in accord with manifesting what you truly need. You may be asking for something which is inauspicious for your soul growth. But ineffective manifestation can also be a sign that you are not putting out your request and then letting it go. Fussing and constant worrying block the process, as does deep emotional investment in the outcome, or following someone else's dream. But this can change!

'Prosperity' tends to focus attention on money, or the lack of it. We worry about future prospects, the ability to support ourselves, finding a job, providing for our old age, attracting abundance and so on. We would be better employed in generating prosperity for ourselves and using our power of intent to enrich our lives. In attracting abundance on all levels and creating an unshakeable sense of well-being and inner enrichment, we are truly wealthy. This doesn't mean you have to be relentlessly positive; you need to examine your underlying beliefs and acknowledge doubts and fears, and then transmute, rather than deny, them. But you always have the choice of taking the positive view.

Using this book

Crystals for Prosperity is not just a book about attracting money. It is both a crystal reference – the Prosperity Stones Compendium and A–Z Directory – and a practical, hands-on guide, with exercises and layouts, to using crystals to enrich your life and exploring what might be blocking your abundance. The Prosperity Stones Compendium and the A–Z Directory assist in choosing your stones. You can wear the crystals you discover, place them in your environment, or lay them out in grids or on your body – and on to the chakras, which can be utilised as a support system for generating abundance.

Merely reading the book won't enrich your life. Doing the exercises and taking a hard look at what you believe about prosperity, and letting go of detrimental patterning will. Journaling tracks those changes and helps you to appreciate your enriched life.

A number of questions are posed to assist you to search deeply into the underlying thoughts and feelings that control how much prosperity – or poverty – you experience. As you will be returning to these answers several times, it would be sensible to keep a notebook in which you record your answers, your experiences, and your successes. Record also which crystals you find most beneficial so that you can use these again in the future – but do check out that they are still valid as, if a block or issue has been lifted, for example, another may need dealing with. It is rather like peeling back the layers until you reach the golden core of abundance within you.

The A-Z Directory offers several crystal options under each heading so that you can identify exactly the right crystal for you. No two people are exactly the same and the more precise you can be in identifying 'your' crystals, the more success you will achieve (see pages 18–23). To work most efficiently, crystals need to be prepared (see pages 24–28) before commencing any ritual or layout.

The crystal layouts are based on sacred geometry, which shapes energy in a specific way to attract, purify and transmute, or radiate as required. Choose whichever shape appeals to you most, or which fits your intention. Layouts are included on which you can place your crystals. But, it could be helpful to purchase a Flower of Life (see page 42) baseboard on which most of the shapes can be laid as this can be left undisturbed in an appropriate place.

Twelve steps to abundance

- Obey the fundamental law of attraction: like follows like.
- Change your mental program: remember what your mind conceives, it achieves.
- Measure your self-worth by who you are, not what you do or what you have.
- Follow your bliss: do what you love and abundance follows.
- Believe you can fulfil your dreams.
- Notice and appreciate all the small joys of everyday life.
- Recognise that the universe wants you to succeed.
- Focus on exactly what you want to attract right now.
- Give yourself time, kindness and compassion.
- Avoid doubt and guilt and no longer procrastinate.
- Let go fear or self-pity.
- Share what you have and take pleasure in the giving.

Start by being you.
The you who is here right now.
In all your power-full beauty.
Manifest the light inside.

And the thirteenth step:

- Lay out an abundance grid (see page 155).

Section I
Crystal Tools

Crystal potency

Earth provides enough to satisfy every man's needs, but not every man's greed.
Mahatma Gandhi

Crystals are potent tools for prosperity and abundance. With their power of attraction and energy generation, they support and amplify your thoughts, feelings and emotions, and attract energy towards you. This means that, when you are working with crystals, you need to be sure that those thoughts, feelings and emotions focus on the positive side of what you want to achieve rather than what you fear might happen or on apparent lack. The same applies if you feel sorry for yourself or feel that the world owes you a living. It is much more productive to believe that you can support yourself in all ways. Be honest with yourself if you do have fears or doubts because you can work with crystals to transmute these into positive feelings and beliefs.

To work at their best, crystals need to be prepared and magnetised. If you ask them specifically to assist in your endeavours, whatever they may be, it avoids any confusion over what a crystal's role in your life is meant to be. But do not limit them. 'This or something better' should be your watchword.

The exercises and layouts in all sections can be adapted for other issues using the crystals in the Compendium or the A–Z Directory.

The abundant universe

The universe is full of magical things patiently waiting for our wits to grow sharper.
Eden Phillpotts

Conceived in the womb of the Earth, Diamonds, Rubies, Sapphires and Emeralds are the most precious of gems and these gifts of the abundant universe have always been worn to signify wealth and status but also had hidden, occult meanings. Not all crystals are bright and shiny, however, and raw stones often work better than faceted for layouts and rituals. Many stones are dull and grainy – something you wouldn't value until you are attuned to their amazing properties. Some are battered and broken, but could still be used to generate well-being. Such crystals have been through the mill and, therefore, have enhanced empathy for your plight. They help you to ferret out underlying causes such as poverty consciousness and past life vows.

Crystal properties are more important than appearance. Many prosperity crystals are semi-precious – opaque chunks of rock – rather than bright and shiny gems. Ancient treasures resemble the night sky, Lapis Lazuli or Azurite; or glow bright red like lifeblood, Carnelian, Red Jasper or Dragon's Blood Jasper. The ancients recognised specific healing, protective and manifestation properties in such crystals. Stones have been continuously used for these purposes, imbuing them with even more potency. Sadly, due to translation problems, we no longer know what *Maziuquez* is, although we do know it assisted in holding on to your possessions in ancient Mesopotamia, Arabia and medieval Spain. The 13th century Lapidary of King Alfonso X the Learned of Spain tells us so. We can, however, use other crystals in the 21st century that have an equally long history together with some exciting new discoveries.

Caring for your crystals

Crystals need care. If your crystals are to work at their best, three things need to happen:

- Choose exactly the right crystal for you as everyone's energy field resonates slightly differently and some stones harmonise well with your energies and others do not. This is why alternative stones are given for specific outcomes. (See page 18.)
- Cleanse the crystal of any vibes it has picked up before coming to you and anything it has drawn to itself while in your possession, and keep it energetically clean and sparkling in the future. (See page 24.)
- Magnetise the crystal or the layout with focused intent so that it attracts to you what you desire for your highest good. If you don't ask a crystal to work with you, it won't know what to do, and if you don't keep its energies topped up, it goes flat exactly like a battery. If you are unclear about your intent, then the crystal is also unclear as to exactly what it is you want it to do. However, crystals have a knack of knowing exactly what you need, rather than what you think you want. So, adding "this or something better" to your magnetising opens the way for something miraculous to manifest. (See page 29.)

So what do crystals do?

Crystals generate, conserve, radiate and amplify energy. They can be powerful attractors. This energy amplification is one of the reasons we instinctively feel good when we hold a crystal that is in tune with our own vibrations. Due to the way the internal crystalline structure of a stone is arranged – its lattice – energy moves slowly or rapidly through the stone or may become trapped within it. Many crystals have a powerful infusion of minerals within their matrix.

Crystals create prosperity by taking your personal intention, potentising, amplifying and sending it out into the universe to attract back all that you wish for. In other words, they appear to work magic but the true source is the extraordinary power of your own thoughts and the attractor factor – of which we hear more shortly.

Aligning with your crystal

The more in tune you are with a crystal, the better the outcome. To align with your crystal's energies:

- *First cleanse your crystal (see page 24).*
- *Hold your crystal, breathe slowly in and out for five breaths, then ask the crystal to show you how it feels to be fully aligned. Remember that this is a feeling that includes a mental state, so do not expect an intellectual answer. Instead pay attention to how you feel. You may well experience yourself moving into energetic*

alignment with energies moving across and around your spine, and then have a sense of going slightly 'up' – indeed, you may lift slightly off your chair or feel the top of your head moving slightly higher.

Everyone experiences this alignment in a way that is unique to them but once you reach it, you know.

Changing the world with intent

Creation's gold mine is in you. The key is deliberate intention. Whatever your dream may be at this moment, identify it. If you cannot define your desire, it can never become a reality.

Mary Manin Morrissey

Intention draws on the power of belief, the written and spoken word, repetition, crystals, the universe, affirmation and letting go. Ancient peoples understood the power of the spoken and written word and of repetition, that's why they chanted spells and incantations. They wore amulets engraved on crystals and let their gods look after the detail.

Intention is your will for something to happen but it's not a forced will, it's an *allowing*. Creating an expansive space. In other words, intention is a way of *being* rather than a way of *doing*. The best space to be in for the exercises, rituals and visualisations in this book is one of relaxed but alert attention and focused intent. The clearer your intention (see pages 16–17), the more quickly what you want manifests. And the more you believe your intention manifests, the more you change your world.

Paradoxically, being unattached to the outcome is equally important. Although all your emotions and feelings are focused in the moment when you carry out a ritual, layout or exercise, they are not intent on an outcome. This is a strange idea to get your head around: needing to be passionately involved and yet be unattached to the outcome. It means, however, that if you get out of the way and let it happen, the universe takes over.

Trying and not trying

So, having an intention is not about *trying* to do something. As Yoda in *Star Wars* pointed out, you either do or you don't. You could *try* your whole life long and not get there. But if you *do,* then you do. It's wise to avoid words such as 'no' and 'not' and 'don't want' when thinking – or *feeling* – about intention. The subconscious mind doesn't understand how putting 'no more' before something such as poverty means that "what I really want is 'abundance'". It just manifests more poverty.

It's also wise not to have an expectation or hidden agenda that 'the world owes me'. This brings in all kinds of negative feelings and hardly creates the right kind of ambience for your intention to manifest. It's far better to have a goal that moves you positively into the right outcome phrased in the present moment. So, "I do/I am/I act/I achieve……" Not, "I am going to……" "I will try to……"

It's also essential to be careful how you phrase your desire. "Give me more" does just that, but it may not be to your benefit or what you expected. If the emotions underlying your intention are unclear, you may well manifest what you craved or feared at your deepest level (see Sections 2 and 3 for assistance on this).

Clarifying intent

Crystals pick up anything and everything you are thinking and feeling – which is why the second and third sections of this book help you to establish how you are affected by your karmic plans and contracts, and your ancestral inheritance; how you view prosperity, what may be blocking you; pinpointing what you are seeking before you start to work with your crystals.

So, before you magnetise a crystal for any of the rituals or layouts that follow, take a few moments to clarify your intent and to ensure that you are holding a positive focus for the outcome. If you have any doubts or fears, work through these with the assistance of a crystal, before you charge up your crystal with intent (see pages 14 and 15).

Putting intention into a crystal

- *Cleanse your crystal.*
- *When you know exactly what your intent is, hold the thought in your mind and feel all the positive emotions associated with manifesting it: joy, fulfilment, excitement, purpose and so on.*
- *Then hold the crystal in your hands, speak your intent out loud and pour your intention and all those good feelings into the crystal as you do so.*
- *Ask the crystal that it takes this intention out to the*

world and manifests it. This magnetises the crystal.

- *Then withdraw your attention.*
- *Place the crystal as appropriate and simply trust that your intention comes into being in the right way and with the right timing.*

Choosing your crystals

Your prosperity crystals need to make your heart sing. You can look through any of my crystal books and see which crystals call out to you, or do the same in a crystal shop. Whatever catches your eye will be good for you. This allows the stones that want to work with you to be attracted towards you. But do note that, if you feel repelled by a crystal, it may be indicating issues you need to deal with.

To choose an individual stone out of several possibilities, put your hand into a tub of crystals and see which one sticks to your fingers, or touch each one and see which one feels good. If you find you can't put a stone down, this is the crystal for you. You can also dowse (see page 19). If you are in any doubt, hold the crystal over your heart, breathe gently and see how it *feels*.

If you're looking for a statement piece, such as an altar stone or one for the wealth corner, the *feeling* of the stone is more important than the look. It should make your heart sing whenever you see it. But it doesn't have to be beautiful or perfect. Sometimes crystals that have been chipped, broken or scratched actually work harder for you than ones that are perfect. Some crystals have 'empathy nicks' that help them to resonate with people's painful feelings and to transmute them.

Choose five crystals from the short directory (see page 209) to be your special prosperity stones. Tumblestones, spheres or flat palmstones are comfortable to handle and radiate energy equally in all directions but you may also want to have a crystal point or two that directs energy in a specific way.

Dowsing for your crystals

You can either use a pendulum when choosing crystals or finger dowse. Both methods use the ability of your intuitive body-mind connection to tune into subtle vibrations and to influence your hands. A focused mind, trust in the process, carefully worded questions and a clear intent support your dowsing and your healing.

Pendulum

If you are familiar with pendulum dowsing, use the pendulum in your usual way. If you are not, this skill is easily learned.

To pendulum dowse

To pendulum dowse, hold your pendulum between the thumb and forefinger of your most receptive hand with about a hand's length of chain hanging down to the pendulum – you will soon learn what is the right length for you. Wrap the remaining chain around your fingers so that it does not obstruct the dowsing.

You will need to ascertain which is a 'yes' and which is a 'no' response. Some people find that the pendulum swings in one direction for 'yes' and at right angles to that axis for 'no', while others have a backwards and forwards swing for one reply, and a circular motion for the other. A 'wobble' of the pendulum can indicate a 'maybe' or that it is not appropriate to dowse at that time, or that the wrong question is being asked. In which case, ask if it is appropriate, and if the answer is 'yes', check that you are framing the question in the correct way. If the pendulum stops completely it is usually inappropriate to ask at that time.

You can ascertain your particular pendulum response by holding the pendulum over your knee and asking: "Is my name [correct name]?" The direction that the pendulum swings will indicate 'yes'. Check by asking: "Is my name [incorrect name]?" to establish 'no'. Or, you can programme in 'yes' and 'no' by swinging the pendulum in a particular direction a few times, saying as you do: "This is yes"; and swinging it in a different direction to programme in 'no'.

To pendulum dowse the best crystal for you

To ascertain which crystal will be most beneficial for you, hold the pendulum in your most receptive hand. Put the forefinger of your other hand on the condition or issue in the A–Z Directory. Slowly run your finger along the list of possible crystals, noting whether you get a 'yes' or 'no' response. Check the whole list to see which 'yes' response is strongest as there may well be several that would be appropriate or you may need to use several crystals in combination. Another way to do this, if you have several of the crystals available, is to touch each crystal in turn, again noting the 'yes' or 'no' response.

If you get a 'no' response when checking out the issue, touch each of the capital letters in turn until you receive a 'yes', then run your finger down the entries until you receive another 'yes'.

How long should you use a crystal?

A pendulum can also be used to establish for how long a crystal should be left in place. This is particularly useful if you are placing the crystal over or around your body or bed, but it can also be helpful if you are wearing a crystal and need to know whether or not to wear it at night – in which case you will get a 'yes' or 'no' answer to the question: "Should I remove this crystal at night?" To establish timing, use an arc on which you have marked five-minute or one-hour or one-day intervals (ask in advance whether the period should be checked in minutes, hours or days). Hold the hand with the pendulum over the centre of the arc and ask that the pendulum will go towards the correct period (see illustration).

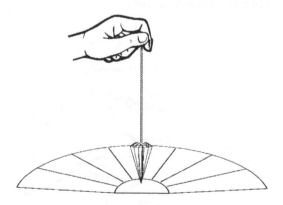

Dowsing over an Arc

Finger Dowsing

Finger dowsing answers 'yes' and 'no' questions quickly and unambiguously, and can be done unobtrusively in situations where a pendulum might provoke unwanted attention. This method of dowsing works particularly well for people who are kinaesthetic, that is to say their body responds intuitively to subtle feelings, but anyone can learn to finger dowse.

To finger dowse

To finger dowse, hold the thumb and first finger of your right hand together (see illustration). Loop the thumb and finger of your left hand through to make a 'chain'. Ask your question clearly and unambiguously – you can speak it aloud or keep it within your mind. Now pull gently but firmly. If the chain breaks, the answer is 'no'. If it holds, the answer is 'yes'.

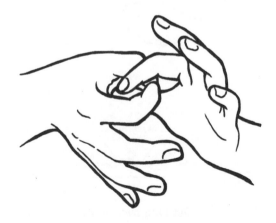

To finger dowse timing

Questions such as "For how long should I leave the crystal/layout in place?" can be answered with a slightly different finger dowsing method, by putting your fingers together and counting. Your fingers will release at the appropriate number. (In other words, the method is reversed so that staying together means 'more time' and releasing indicates the correct amount of time.) Although, you could follow up a 'yes' answer with the question "And longer?" to ascertain whether further time may be appropriate.

First, ask whether the period required is hours, days, weeks or months. When you have ascertained the answer, slot your fingers together and ask that they will hold until the right answer is reached and then release. You can then ask, "1 minute, 2 minutes" and so on, or 1 hour/day/month until you have a definitive answer. You could also dowse over a calendar if the period is weeks rather than days.

Cleansing your crystals

As soon as you get your crystals home, or have gathered your crystal collection together, they need to be cleansed. Proprietary crystal cleansers are excellent as they transmute negative energy the crystal has picked up and then recharge them, but you can do the same with water, sound or brown rice. Tumbled stones and single point crystals are easily cleansed under running water or in salt water (but see the caveat below). Crystal clusters or fragile stones need care as water can easily penetrate the cracks and loosen individual points or layers. These are best placed in brown rice overnight.

Regularly cleanse all your crystals.

Methods:

Running water

Hold your crystals in running water, or pour bottled water over them, or place them in a stream or the ocean to draw off negative energy (use a bag to hold small crystals). It is often recommended that you immerse appropriate crystals in a bowl of water into which a handful of sea salt or rock salt has been added. Salt is best avoided if the crystal is layered or friable, however, see below. Dry the crystal carefully afterwards and place in the sun to re-energize or use a proprietary crystal recharging essence.

Salt – *use with caution*

Salt – and Halite – also draws off toxic energies but may be damaging to layered or friable crystals. You could use salt dissolved in water or seawater, but do so with caution. If using salt, brush it off carefully and make sure that it has been completely removed from any niches or cracks in the crystal as otherwise it will absorb water in the future and could cause splintering. Salt is best used in a 'salt-ring' around the crystal. Or place the crystal on a chunk of Halite.

Rice

Place your crystal in brown rice overnight and then compost the rice (do not eat it). Brown rice seems to have a special affinity with crystals that have been subjected to EMF or negative energy pollution, rapidly drawing it off. Place the crystals in the sun or under the moon to re-energize if appropriate or use a crystal essence (see page 27 and Resources).

Sound

Sound tuning forks, bells, tingshaws, a Tibetan bowl or gong over the crystal to cleanse it and then recharge in sun or moonlight.

Crystals

Large crystals such as Carnelian, Smoky Quartz or Citrine can cleanse another crystal, but will need cleansing themselves afterwards.

Returning to the earth

You will need to dowse to establish the length of time a crystal needs to return to the earth in order to cleanse and recharge as the period will differ with each crystal. If you do not have a garden, a flowerpot filled with soil or sand can be used instead. If you bury crystals to cleanse them, remember to mark the spot.

Smudging

Sage, sweetgrass or joss sticks are excellent for smudging as they quickly remove negative energies. Light the smudge stick and pass it over the crystal if it is large, or hold the crystal in your hand in the smoke if it is small. It is traditional to fan the smoke gently with a feather but this is not essential.

Visualising light

Hold your crystal in your hands and visualise a column of bright white light coming down and covering the crystal, absorbing anything negative it may have picked up and restoring the pure energy once more. If you find visualisation difficult, you can use the light of a candle. Crystals also respond well to being placed in sun or moonlight to cleanse and recharge.

Crystal clearing essences

A number of crystal and space clearing essences are available from essence suppliers, crystal shops and the Internet (see Resources). Personally I never move far without Petaltone Clear2Light, a crystal and space clearing essence, and Petaltone Z14, an etheric clearer. But you can also make your own (see below and *Crystal Prescriptions volume 7*). Either drop the essence directly on to the crystal, gently rubbing it over the crystal with your finger, or put a few drops into clean spring water in an atomiser or spray bottle and gently mist the crystal.

Make your own crystal cleansing essence
Choose one or two from the list and combine in an essence. (See Crystal Prescriptions volume 7. *You can also add recharging crystals, see below.)*

Cleansing/Clearing crystals: Amber, Black Amber, Black Tourmaline, Blue or Black Kyanite, Citrine (natural), Flint, Halite, Hanksite, Hematite, Shungite, Smoky Quartz.

Re-Energizing your crystals
Some of the proprietary crystal cleansers also re-energize the stones but all crystals benefit from being out in sunlight for a few hours to recharge, and white stones enjoy bathing in moonlight. Or, you can spritz them with a recharging essence.

Recharging: Anandalite™, Carnelian, Citrine, Golden Healer, Orange Kyanite, Quartz, Red Jasper, Selenite, Sunstone.

Dedicating your crystals

Once your crystal has been cleansed and energized, it needs to be dedicated to working for your highest good. Hold the crystal in your hands for a few moments to attune to it, then ask it to always work with you for your highest good and to help you enjoy an abundant life. If you have a specific task for the crystal to assist with, state it clearly and precisely to magnetise the crystal or layout (see below).

Magnetising your crystals

Crystal energy is powerful but so too is the extraordinary ability of your mind to create. Together, they are a magnet for whatever you wish to attract. You become co-creators. The power of your mind works through language, images and beliefs which interact with crystals to co-create your world. But crystals also work with your mind and emotions, and harnessing emotions to your intention amps up the energy even further. Indeed, without strongly *feeling* your intention, little is likely to change (see pages 14–17). When seeking prosperity you need to feel it, taste it, smell it. In other words, put your whole being and all your senses into manifesting it through the crystal. But, as we have seen, keeping up that level of input is counterproductive. Once the intent is set up, let go. Leave the crystal to do its work.

Always remember to magnetise your crystals before using them for rituals or layouts.

Storing your crystals

Crystals prefer to be out there working rather than being shut away, but sometimes even the most willing crystal needs a rest, or your priorities change. Always cleanse a crystal before putting it away and, if you no longer need it to perform a specific task, tell the crystal so, thanking it for its work on your behalf, and ask it to continue to support your well-being. While crystals that are not working enjoy sunlight for a day or two, this will fade the colour so it is sensible not to leave them on window ledges or in direct sunlight.

Similarly, crystals can be damaged by being left outdoors so do check yours regularly if outside – if you are leaving crystals outdoors rough pieces are less susceptible to damage. Your bigger crystals enjoy being displayed on shelves so that you luxuriate in their beauty, and smaller crystals can be wrapped or placed in a mandala or other pleasing layout in a suitable place.

Keep your five prosperity crystals together in a pouch when not in use, carefully wrapping any points and store them in the wealth corner of a room (see page 145).

Disconnection from a grid

If your crystal has been working with a specific intent and especially within a grid, it makes sense to clear that intent before putting the crystal away.

To disconnect from a crystal or grid

- *Gather up the crystal(s).*
- *Thank them for the work they have been doing for you. If appropriate, ask that they will go on assisting in the best way possible.*
- *Cleanse the crystal(s) thoroughly and, if appropriate, put them out in the sun or moonlight (white crystals) to recharge.*
- *Wrap the crystals and put them in a drawer or box until next required.*

Crystal shapes for generating prosperity

Quartz shapes

Quartz is the most abundant crystal on the planet. The major prosperity stone, Citrine, is a form of Quartz, as is the love attractor Rose Quartz and the Smoky Quartz that assists in manifesting your dreams. Amethyst is also a Quartz. Some of the alchemicalised Aura Quartzes, which have precious metals bonded to their surface, assist with manifesting your dreams of abundance. Candle Quartz, which looks like melted wax, or Spirit Quartz, which has sharper points, draw abundance to a group. Ideal for holding intention, Quartz's ability to amplify energy is truly awesome. Focusing concentration, Quartz takes energy back to its most perfect state, removing negative conditioning or toxic thought patterns. Four of its natural forms are particularly appropriate for increasing your prosperity and are especially suitable for placing in the wealth corner of your home (see page 145):

Generator

Large generator crystal: Six-sided top facet. This particular generator is double-terminated, which breaks old patterns.

Generator cluster, several long crystals attached at the base, ideally springing from the same matrix.

Generator crystals come in two shapes. A single generator point, natural or artificially shaped, has six equal facets meeting in a point at the top and has often been cut so that it stands point up. This shape increases your inner resources. All single generators project energy out and increase your core energy. Small single generator points draw energy in to enhance your prosperity.

A generator cluster has long points radiating out in all directions, each of which creates and projects energy. Such a cluster can be magnetised to bring about several outcomes as it puts energy into all your endeavours equally. Use a generator cluster to heal discord within yourself, your family or a group that is preventing you from living an enriched life.

Abundance

Abundance crystal

With many small crystals clustering around the base of a large crystal, Abundance crystals are excellent if you want to attract wealth into your home but they attract many other forms of prosperity too. Magnetise one to bring you good fortune, good friends and a good life.

Manifestation

Manifestation crystal with small inner crystals.

A manifestation crystal is a crystal-within-a-crystal. One, or more, small crystals totally enclosed by a larger crystal, although those with inclusions or phantoms are sometimes sold as manifestation crystals. Manifestations are rare but you may find one in a batch of Quartz points. Creative Manifestation crystals amplify your thoughts and intentions and can be magnetised to manifest anything which would enhance your life, such as joy or artistic ability or contact with guides and mentors. However, these crystals can be literal in how your desire is interpreted. Use these wonderful treasures wisely after careful contemplation of what you truly intend.

Crystal prosperity shapes other than Quartz

Natural spiral

Ammonite/Ammolite shell (see page 40).

Shiva Shell

A spiral draws abundance to you (see page 40).

Grids and layouts

Crystals laid on background grids harness the power of sacred geometry to amplify crystal power. You can use a template for this – see below – or place the crystals in the shape on a background cloth. The cloth can be a colour that harmonises with your intention (see page 14).

Grids create an energetic pattern that is both contained within the grid and radiates out beyond it. If you are creating a grid to attract abundance, lay your first crystal at the outermost end pointing in. If you are creating a grid to manifest and radiate abundance out into your environment, start at the centre of the grid, pointing out.

The Square and the Rectangle

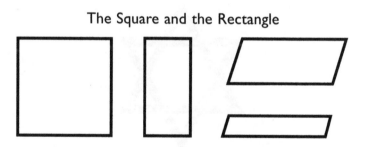

Square, rectangle and parallelograms

Squares and rectangles consolidate energy and create a boundary. They are particularly useful if you want to hold on to your assets or consolidate work. The square template is one of the most basic and versatile of grids. A configuration with perfect symmetry, it anchors intention and grounds energy. In its simplest form, it is a crystal placed in four corners of a room or around a bed. But it creates an energetic cube. It can be used to grid a building, or be placed around a specific site. A protective layout, the square consolidates energy, balancing and solidifying it. A square grid also repels detrimental energies and so creates a contained, safe space. If appropriate the grid can be extended by placing anchoring crystals outside the square. This holds grid energy in place for long periods of time and is particularly useful if you are gridding a house. Place anchor stones on the outside of the corners and grid crystals on the corner.

Hexagram

Hexagram

Known as 'the Creator's Star', 'Star of David' or 'Solomon's Seal', the hexagram is an ancient symbol of protection and the unification of opposing forces. The symbol for the heart chakra is a hexagram. It draws in and then consolidates and anchors energy. Place crystals on the external points, and on the intersections if appropriate.

Pentangle

Upright pentangle, reversed pentangle

A pentangle (pentagram) draws the assistance of the gods – the archetypal, universal forces – from 'above' down to 'below': infusing projects on the Earth with creative and protective power. The reversed pentangle grounds energy and spirit into the earth plane. Neither has an innate connection to the dark side, contrary to what superstitious people may say. It is intention and purpose that give a grid its 'good' or 'not-good' power, not the shape of the grid itself. The upward point represents spirit, the other four points the elements of earth, air, fire and water. The pentangle unites these. Place grid crystals on the points, and on the intersections if appropriate.

The Spiral

Spiral (a spiral can be left- or right-handed).

A spiral is one of the foundational forms in which organisms grow. It creates vortex energy and is a basis for accelerating progress and switching on positive growth. Depending on which way a crystal is placed, a spiral draws energy down into its centre – a crystal placed at the top begins the process – or radiates it from a crystal placed at the centre. When joining the crystals do not go back to the first crystal laid. Instead, spiral the energy out and away or down into the centre. A multi-armed spiral can also be used.

Multi-armed Spiral or Sunburst

 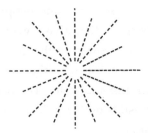

Multi-armed spiral   **Sunburst**

A multi-armed spiral, or a sunburst layout, is highly energizing, radiating that energy over a large area. It is particularly suited to placing on the ground or over a map. Although it is usual to start in the centre and work outwards, it can be helpful to dowse for the placements as a central alignment may need to be set out first, or last, with the crystals placed to draw energy in or out. The layout can always be adjusted later to fine-tune the energies. This layout is not activated by joining with a wand to complete the circuit as the intention is to radiate the energy as widely as possible. It is set in motion by the intention of your mind. When placing the crystals, remember that points channel energy in the direction they face so direct a point towards the next spot on a layout. If a point is facing towards you or to a specific spot, it channels energy in to you or to that spot. If pointing away from you it sends energy outwards.

Triple Spiral (Triskelion)

Triskelion

The triple spiral is a dynamic symbol of activation,

movement and expansion in contrast to all that is fixed and unmoving. It is a cyclical grid: life moving forward. Use the triple spiral if you need to draw dynamic energy into a situation or to infuse it with light. You can also use it to shift blocks. It is the perfect grid to move through transition phases of life. The grid can also be used as 'past', 'present' and 'future' – lay one spiral, beginning at the centre, at a time to get to the bottom of an issue, the second to bring about insight and change, and then the third to integrate the change and move it forward. A keystone placed in the centre integrates the grid.

The Flower of Life

Flower of Life within a circular border

Depicting the circles and cycles of the cosmic mind, the

Flower of Life is as old as time itself. It encompasses the geometry of both time and space – and the foundational building blocks of life. The Flower contains within itself the Seed of Life, the Fruit of Life, the Vesica Piscis, the Tree of Life, the Merkaba, Metatron's Cube – and the Platonic solids. All of which can be outlined by crystals placed on the Flower.

Metatron's Cube

Metatron's Cube

Metatron's Cube is a complex, multidimensional connector arising from the Flower of Life. It plots the four cardinal directions plus 'above' and 'below'. The Cube was used by the alchemists of old as a vehicle for creation – or for containment. It is said to be a map of creation, plotting the 'big bang' and the ever unfolding energy that rippled out from that event. But, rather than being a map of a single universe, it is a map of the multi-verse: the finite and infinite possible universes, including the universe in which we live and the natural and super-natural worlds. The notion of a multiverse expands space-time and goes right down to the quantum level of creation. When laying a Metatron grid, place crystals in the circles. You can add crystals along the connecting lines if appropriate.

The Labyrinth

Labyrinth

The Labyrinth is one of the oldest grids in existence. It takes many forms, but all share the core design, a winding pathway leading from the outer edge to the centre. Unlike a maze, a Labyrinth has no dead ends or blind alleys. Although it twists and turns, ultimately it leads to the central point and then out again. The Labyrinth is a journey of discovery through the passage of time and into your deepest self. It encompasses change, growth, progress and transformation. The Labyrinth continually expands your vision of what is possible and what your soul intended for you on your pathway through life. It assists you to see clearly and to listen deeply. When you walk the sacred Labyrinth, or lay crystals from the outside in, you walk into your inner core. It takes you into wholeness and centeredness, helping you to be grounded around that core.

Tree of Life/Ancestral Tree

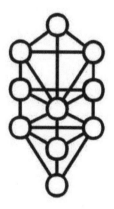

Tree of Life

The Tree of Life arises from the centre of the Flower of Life. Or, in the Celtic understanding, it is drawn as a tree with the roots deep in the Earth and the branches reaching up to heaven with the trunk uniting them. In some Celtic forms, the branches and the roots also meet. The Tree of Life can be stretched and expanded to cover the human body or an area in the environment. It is the perfect grid for healing the ancestral line. The Tree of Life layout quickly purifies, balances and re-energizes all the chakras, shifting blocks to prosperity and creativity as it does so. When laying the grid, place crystals in the circles. You can also place crystals along the connecting lines if appropriate.

[Information extracted from *Crystal Grids*.]

Joining up a layout

When you have laid out your shape in crystals, use a crystal wand (a long, straight pointed or gently rounded crystal, or a long, flat-bladed crystal), or the power of your mind to join up the underlying geometric shape. Remember to go back to the first point to complete the shape – unless you are creating a spiral.

Anchoring the grid

An anchor stone grounds the energetic grid produced by a geometric layout into physical and material reality. Place it to the side or around the grid.

Anchoring Stones: Black Tourmaline, Flint, Hematite, Smoky Quartz.

Collecting the energy: the Keystone

A crystal such as Quartz placed in the centre of a grid 'gathers' the energy into itself harnessing the power of attraction. It then radiates the energy as required and is useful for keeping in a pocket or the wealth corner to continue the manifesting properties of the grid.

Creating a 'holding-space'

When toxic thoughts, beliefs or emotions have been drawn off, a 'holding-space' crystal fills the resulting energetic 'hole' with light to allow time for a new, beneficial pattern to be inputted. It is said that Nature abhors a vacuum and this is very much the case when something toxic has been released from the etheric body and the spaces between the cells in your physical body, or your chakras. Crystals fill the space with 'light' energy rather than something heavy and anti-abundance. Many crystals, such as Anandalite, Calcite or Brandenberg Amethyst, fulfil both purposes. When laying grids around yourself, place a 'holding-space' crystal at the top of your head to hold the space for a new program to be inputted, and balance it with a grounding crystal at your feet.

The chakras and abundance

The chakras are the keys to the life you are meant to live, one of joy, love, connection and abundance on all levels.
Jules Blythe, *The Root Chakra Challenge: A Healing & Balancing Toolkit*

The chakras are multilayered, multidimensional vortexes of subtle energy that radiate several feet out all around your physical body. (See *Crystal Prescriptions volume 4.*) Linkage points between the physical and subtle energy bodies, they are metaphysical energy portals, rather than physical, but they are essential to our efficient functioning in the world and to raising consciousness. Chakras mediate how much you take in from the world around you, and govern your response to that outer world.

You can use these subtle energy centres to support your prosperity. Certain issues, such as poverty consciousness, self-pity or a lack of basic security, pertain to specific chakras (see page 54), and by placing crystals on the appropriate chakras you transmute the negative issue into positive prosperity consciousness. Stones have also long been linked to the organs of the body and can be placed over those organs to transmute negative feelings associated with them: fear with the kidneys, anger with the liver, grief with the lungs, lack of sweetness in life with the pancreas, and so on.

Blocked chakras are reflected in personalities. 'Mean

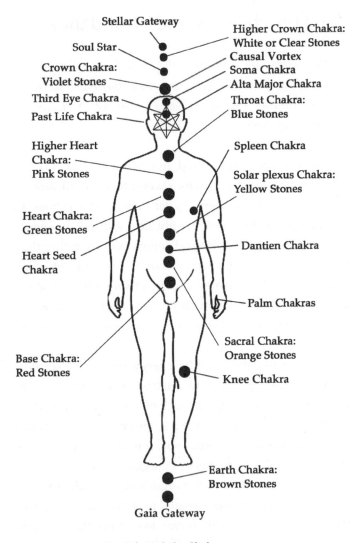

Crystals and the Chakras

and grasping' or 'poor me' personalities most often result from lower chakra or heart blockages. The chakras in the head function on a mental and intuitive basis and thoughts are powerful manifestors – or blockers. Both the past life chakras (behind the ears) and the causal vortex (above and to the side of the head) hold karmic and ancestral memories and attitudes. Those above and around the head are spiritual connection points although the soma chakra (mid-hairline) and the heart seed chakra (below the breastbone) are both points where the soul and spirit attach.

The A–Z Directory has suggestions as to which chakra(s) would be suitable to deal with underlying issues affecting your prosperity consciousness – or lack of it.

Your manifestation (palm) chakras

As we have seen, there are far more than the seven 'traditional' chakras. Two so-called 'minor' chakras are firmly attached to the earth plane and are far from minor in their effect. Activating these chakras assists the manifestation process and enhances your ability to project energy out to the world or to receive it.

The manifestation chakras are what we use to *sense* crystal energies but these chakras are also part of the manifestation process. They are receptive: receiving energy. And expressive: radiating it. So, they are intimately connected with your ability to receive and to generate. The phrase 'tight-fisted' means exactly that. The manifestation chakras are tightly closed. There is no flow.

You can soon have these powerful energy points working for you. The manifestation chakras are in the centre of your palms and radiate into your fingers, wrists and lower arms. If you rub your hands together briskly and then bring them together with fingers steepled and palms almost touching, you can feel the chakras tingling and pulsating. It is as though there is a ball of energy between your palms.

To open the manifestation chakras:

- *State your intention of opening the manifestation chakras.*
- *Rapidly open and close your fingers five or six times.*

- *Concentrate your attention into your right-hand palm and then your left. (If you are left-handed reverse the process.) Picture them opening like petals. The centres will become hot and energized.*

- *Bring your hands together. Stop as soon as you feel the energy of the two chakras meeting.*

- *If you brought your hands together with fingers touching, reverse them so that your hands point in opposite directions. Place your right and then your left above the other. You'll soon learn to recognise what works for you.*

- *With a little practice you'll be able to open the chakras simply by putting your attention there.*

- *Place a crystal point on your hand. Feel the energies radiating into your palm. Turn the point towards your arm and then towards your fingers. Sense the direction of the energy flow. (Points channel energy in the direction they face.)*

The benefits

Fully functioning manifestation chakras help you to receive energy from the universe – or crystals – and channel this into your energy field. They also assist in putting out intention to the universe. Your creativity flows, manifestation becomes a continual process of receiving and giving out.

Chakra abundance issues

Each chakra has prosperity challenges, gifts and associations depending on whether it is open or closed.

Gaia Gateway: A higher resonance of the earth star, this chakra anchors high frequency light into the physical body and the body of the Earth. Without this chakra high vibrational energy cannot be assimilated and grounded. When your Gaia gateway is open and functioning at optimum, you are aware of being a part of a sacred whole, part of the energy system of the Earth and, at the same time, All That Is. When this chakra is blocked, there is an inability to ground and connect with higher energies. Disconnection from the Earth as a sacred, living being may lead to greed and over-utilisation of the planet's resources and consequent disregard for others who share the planet.

Earth Star: The earth star chakra connects you to the Earth's core as well as its electromagnetic fields and energy meridians. This chakra helps you to bring things into concrete form, grounding and anchoring new frequencies and actualising your plans and dreams. It is a place of safety and regeneration. Without it, you will have only a toehold in incarnation, and be physically and psychologically ungrounded. With it, you have a stable, calm and strong centre from which to handle the vicissitudes of life and its pleasures with equal composure.

When this chakra is functioning well you are grounded and comfortable in incarnation. You will be practical and operate well in everyday reality. When it is blocked, you are ungrounded and impractical, unable to manifest your unrealistic goals.

Knee: When working well the knee chakras ensure you are flexible and able to adapt to changing circumstances. Literally able to 'go with the flow' and yet having perseverance when required. You are able to use your willpower to manifest a desired outcome rather than to insist on it. These chakras ensure that you have the ability to nurture and support yourself and manifest what you need on a day-to-day basis. When the knee chakras are balanced, you can set realistic goals and outcomes, and let go when appropriate. There is an ability to move forward with confidence, well grounded and practical. Basic needs are fulfilled with ease. A blown knee chakra constantly meets problems with authority, authority figures and bureaucracy. Someone with blocked knee chakras experiences a lack of basic sustenance, materially and nutritionally. Needs are not met and so you are focused on what is lacking rather than what is there. The soul is not grounded into the earth plane, or practical everyday reality, and so feels empty.

Palm: Hands are powerful sensors, part of a continual process of receiving and giving out. They assist you to interact with the world on an energetic level. The palm chakras are both receptive: receiving and sensing energy, and expressive: radiating and channelling it. So, they are intimately connected with your ability to receive and to generate, manifest and *actualise*. Fully functioning palm chakras help you to receive energy from the universe – or from crystals – and channel this into your energy field. But they also project energy. This is where you experience expanded awareness and increased creativity in the physical and subtle energy worlds. When these chakras are blocked, grasping greed and numbness are present. Closed off and withdrawn from society, antisocial, but paradoxically needy without knowing the reason why. There is an inability to receive, including a refusal to ask for help or accept it when offered.

Base: The base chakra is linked to your core energy and to your connection to Earth. It is the foundation for all the other chakras along the spine, a secure base on which they rest. It represents both your home and your career: your place in the world. When it functions well you are grounded and connected to your core. The base chakra is also the area of the will to survive and the ability to make things happen. This is where you discover yourself as an individual and take responsibility for yourself. It is where you recognise the tribe to which you belong and where you feel safe, or where ancestral issues create insecurity. When this chakra is functioning well, you trust the universe. Imbalances here lead to feelings of stuckness, anger, impotence and frustration – and the inability to let go.

Sacral: The Sanskrit name for this chakra means 'one's own base'. This creative chakra is an important part of your core energy system and affects your ability to bring things into manifestation. It also assists you to hold your boundaries steady. It has a great deal to do with how you handle your immediate environment and matters such as money, career and authority figures. When this chakra is working well you experience yourself as a dynamic agent of change in your life. When this chakra is functioning well you are able to give and receive in equal measure. When it is not, you may feel unsupported, shut off from nurturing and sharing, or feel jealous and possessive.

Dantien: The dantien is an energy vortex and storage vault rather than a chakra *per se*. It is a place of inner strength, stability and balance. A powerpoint, the dantien is the point of balance for the physical body, where lifeforce is stored and your body earthed. Acting like a reservoir, this is your core energy source. When you are connected to your core, you not only have more physical energy as you are not affected by life's ups and downs, but you are also more emotionally stable and better able to resist stress. You are not easily thrown off balance. Nor are you open to manipulation by other people. When the dantien is full, you have inner resources to draw on. You are literally power-full.

Solar Plexus: This chakra can have a powerful effect on your ability to assert yourself. The solar plexus represents radiant self-confidence and self-esteem – and your ability to laugh at yourself and the world. When functioning well it acts as a point of equilibrium between your present soul purpose and your past karma so that previous learning is applied. When this chakra is too open other people can all too easily draw on your energy and deplete you. Their emotions will rush into your subtle and physical bodies, overwhelming you with their feelings so that you lose track of your own. Your boundaries are diffuse. It is difficult to know where you end and someone else begins, which leads to people-pleasing rather than expressing your authentic self. When it is blocked, there will be a sense of inferiority and a tendency to cling too tightly – or to push other people away. Intimacy and sharing are impossible when this chakra is blocked.

Spleen: When the spleen chakra is wide open, other people can draw on your energy, leaving you depleted. If you have a constant ache under your left armpit then the chakra is too open and a psychic vampire has hooked in to get their energy fix. People can easily take advantage of you, manipulating and coercing you into self-destructive actions that are not for your highest good. If the chakra is balanced, energy can easily flow around your physical and subtle bodies, and you are protected. When the chakra is blocked, emotional energy especially anger can become stuck there, and this will also deplete you. You will feel rootless, purposeless, exhausted and manipulated, and powerless.

Heart Seed: The heart seed creates a connection to who you really are. It helps you to recall the reason for incarnation, encouraging you to be in spiritual service to humanity. Opening this chakra connects you to your soul purpose and how it fits into the overall divine plan. It facilitates activating the karmic tools you have available to actualise your soul potential. When the heart seed chakra is blown heart energy and compassion cannot be integrated and expended appropriately. Blockage results in depletion and exhaustion from being overly compassionate, giving without consideration as to whether this is necessary or appropriate. It can also result in the martyr who feels hard done by, or in victimhood as others take advantage. *(See the Karpman Triangle page 97.)*

Heart: The heart chakra is the core of your being: where the physical and the spiritual energies fuse and unconditional love thrives and is shared with others. It is the site of the bonds you make with other people, your relationships, and your interaction with the wider worlds around you. Unlimited, it is connected to 'All that Is'. When your heart chakra is open, you 'live from your heart' feeling safe and, therefore, compassionate. This is the basis of altruism, generosity and kindness – and respect for others. An open heart knows there will always be enough. It nurtures and shares – although it knows how to say 'no' and to keep appropriate boundaries. A closed heart suffers from poverty consciousness and egocentricity.

Higher Heart: Connected to ancestral DNA and to the past life patterning you carry in your body, if this chakra is blocked old patterns will hold sway and you will find it difficult to break away from family expectations.

Throat: This chakra is where you express yourself, including strongly felt feelings and emotions that come from the heart or solar plexus chakra, as well as thoughts. If it is blocked and there is no outlet for these feelings and thoughts, it can lead to speaking what you think others wish to hear rather than being honest and sharing your heartfelt truth. You may feel that you have no right to express an opinion or to receive. If the chakra is functioning well you will freely express those opinions and be prepared to enter into debate about them, and compromise or adjust with ease when appropriate. But you will also be able to stick to your principles when necessary. This chakra has a surprising amount to do with willpower and the choices that arise in life. It mediates our contact with the external world.

Third Eye (brow): The brow chakra is where your inner sight meets your outer sight and bonds into intuitive insight. When this chakra is functioning well it connects to guides, mentors and higher beings. It helps you to see beyond consensual reality into what really *is*. Opening your third eye can make your life smoother, but discretion is needed to ensure that it really is functioning at optimum and not accessing a level that is based on wishful thinking and illusion. An overactive brow can create a tendency to live in an escapist fantasy world, with a distorted view of reality. This is the overactive imagination going full-steam ahead without constraint. Such rapid thought patterns lead to being spaced out, or to having a one-track mind. It can result in uncontrolled contact with other, apparent, dimensions of reality as there is no filtering or discrimination as to what is perceived psychically. A blocked third eye leads to a lack of vision. There may be unhealthy attachment to a belief system. Narrow-mindedness, fear and cynicism are some of the consequences of a blocked third eye. You may be forgetful, an obsessive worrier or constantly doubting. It leads to ultra-linear rational thought or to muddled thinking with no ability to integrate insight and intuition with the intellect. The viewpoint is narrow and imagination may be severely impaired, so there will be problems with visualisation. Blockages often occur in this chakra from childhood if you have been discouraged from speaking about what you see – physically or metaphysically – or from following your own inner guidance. This quickly leads to self-doubt and a lack of trust in your intuition. When this occurs there is a fear of success and 'imposter syndrome' (fear of being found out as not being who or as capable as you purport to be) is common.

Soma: A higher resonance of the third eye, when activated the soma chakra opens metaphysical awareness and visionary ability. It has to do with perception of the cycles of time and awareness of the workings of synchronicity. When this chakra is functioning well it gives you the mental clarity necessary to achieve en-lighten-ment.

Crown: The crown chakra is the place of spiritual, intellectual and intuitive *knowing* so that you understand what is around you on many levels. It connects to multi-dimensions and multiverses. There can be no spiritual connection when this chakra is blocked. No interaction with your own higher self either, leading to feeling like an outsider or imposter. You will be indecisive, suffering from chronic exhaustion or excess frustration as you never seem to be getting anywhere in your spiritual search. You will have a blocked sense of power, leading to negative egotism.

Past Life: The past life chakras are where you store the memories of your previous lives, deeply ingrained soul programs, and emotional baggage from the past. They hold all the traumas, dramas, gifts and lessons you have learned over many lifetimes and may well be holding on to outdated soul intentions from previous lives. This elongated dual chakra links to the karmic blueprint which has the soul wounds, physical and emotional, from the past embedded in it but can also help you to reconnect to soul gifts that you have developed in the past. Blockages here mean that you are stuck in the past and cannot move forward. You may well be repeating your own past life patterns or recreating ancestral patterns that have been passed down through your family.

Causal Vortex: Acting rather like a universal and cosmic worldswide web, the causal vortex accesses the Akashic Records especially that of your own soul and your ancestors. It assists in assessing how far you have travelled on your spiritual journey and how well you are doing with your karmic lessons – and holds a record of these. Cause and effect is understood dispassionately when viewed from the perspective of this chakra. There is no emotional involvement. When activated, it ensures that the connection to your soul is open and helps you access your karmic skills and abilities. It keeps the mind clear and focused, allowing soul input, ideas and intuition to flow freely.

Alta Major: When balanced, the alta major gives the ability to see the bigger picture. All the pieces of the jigsaw puzzle of life fit in place. It enhances intuitive ideas and makes them more solid, tangible and achievable. This chakra holds valuable information about our ancestral past and the ingrained patterns that govern human life and awareness. It, in conjunction with the causal vortex and past life chakras, contains your past life karma and the contractual agreements you made with your higher self and others before incarnating in this lifetime. Activating it enables you to read your soul's plan. When this chakra is blocked, memories of the past will be clung to and will govern behaviour.

Soul Star: This chakra also holds the collective karma of humankind and the history of the evolution of the cosmos. An interface for relationship with the universe and beyond, the soul star is a bridge between spirit and matter. This chakra adjusts extremely high spiritual frequencies so they can be integrated into matter. When assimilated by the physical body, they can be expressed here on Earth. If this chakra is blocked, there is little or no awareness of being an eternal spirit who happens to be in physical incarnation at the present time, and equally no connection to higher beings or to your own higher energies. The viewpoint is consequentially narrow, materialistic and greedy or needy. You may well feel that you have no right to exist at all and constantly apologise for yourself. Unresolved past life issues and previous soul imperatives may well be ruling your life.

Stellar Gateway: The stellar gateway is a dimensional portal rather than a physical site. It is a point of connection to the divine and to the multiverses surrounding us: where the soul can make a connection to its own higher self, other realms, higher dimensions and All That Is. When this chakra is imbalanced the soul will be fragmented, disintegrated, unable to function in the everyday world. A blocked stellar gateway means you are unable to connect to the soul or higher dimensions. There is a feeling that the material realm is all that there is and so spiritual qualities such as empathy and compassion are lacking and ego runs rife.

[For further information on the chakras see Crystal Prescriptions 4.*]*

'Traditional' chakra colours

A tradition has grown up linking chakras with specific colours. Although there are other options, you can use these chakra-colour combinations when choosing crystals to release chakra blockages or deal with issues.

Chakra	Colour
Earth Star	brown, dark grey, maroon
Knee	multicoloured, tan
Base	red
Sacral	orange
Dantien	reddish-orange, amber
Solar Plexus	yellow, light greenish yellow
Spleen	green
Heart Seed	pale pearlescent blue, pink, white
Heart	green/pink
Higher Heart	pink, gold, purple, blue
Palm	silver-white, golden-white, red, blue
Throat	blue, turquoise
Third Eye	indigo
Soma	blue, lavender, white, ultraviolet
Crown	white, purple, lavender
Stellar Gateway	deep violet, white, gold, silver or clear
Soul Star	magenta, white, black
Alta Major	magenta, green
Causal Vortex	white, gold, violet
Gaia Gateway	black, brown, silver, gold

[For further information on the chakras see Crystal Prescriptions 4.*]*

If your crystals aren't working

Remember that it's always possible for a specific crystal to never be a proper vibrational match for you. If you find that's the case consider regifting it back to the earth or even regifting it to someone else.

Hibiscus Moon

If you've followed all the steps – including those in the next sections – but nothing is working for you, check out:

- Have you properly cleansed and magnetised your crystals?
- Have you chosen the right crystals for you?
- Have you really uncovered your deepest thoughts and feelings around prosperity?
- Have you used Feng Shui principles to check out your location – see page 147 and *Crystal Prescriptions 5* for the effects of 'arrows', roads pointing at your house etc?
- Are ancestral expectations – or the jealousy of others – getting in the way? (In which case you need ancestral healing and psychic protection, see *Crystal Prescriptions 5* and 6.)

Finally, there is one last thing to check out:
Are you living in an area of geopathic or electromagnetic stress?

Both geopathic stress (GS), which includes 'black ley

lines' and other environmental disturbances, and electro-magnetic frequencies (EMFs) can seriously affect both health and prosperity (see *Crystal Prescriptions 3*). You may need to take appropriate crystal precautions to create a safe, EMF or geopathic stress-free space in which to set up a grid.

Section 2

Choosing To Be You

Who are you?

To live is to choose. But to choose well, you must know who you are and what you stand for, where you want to go and why you want to get there.
Kofi Annan

You are your greatest asset. But you may also be your own worst enemy. Everyone is conditioned, to a larger or smaller extent, by what has gone before and, for many people, what the future is *expected* to hold. Though we can never know exactly what that may be, of course. We are also conditioned by our role in the family – which carries over into society and the outside world. Ancestral programming, parental expectations and trying to conform to what you *think* the world expects of you is one of the strongest blocks to abundance. As Salma Hayek pointed out: "If you enjoy the process, it's your dream. If you are enduring the process, just desperate for the result, it's somebody else's dream."

Think, feel and desire abundance for yourself, not for someone else's version of what abundance should be.

A large part of reaching physical and spiritual maturity is to become Self-sufficient. To find your own true Self – and identify your purpose in life.

As a karmic astrologer, I have counselled many people who have gone into a particular job because the family, or society, thought they weren't good enough to do anything else and so didn't encourage taking a risk. Or, it was the 'safe option', or because the family simply pushed for material success above all else. Sometimes there was an unfinished karmic carryover to be dealt with. There is little satisfaction at any level in such a, seeming, life choice. It is actually made from an imperative – that is, an unconscious program running deep below the surface. It is very different to a choice made from a free heart and mind. As a corollary, I also look at the charts of people who have broken out, only to feel exiled from their own community as a result because of their own, or those around them's beliefs and expectations *even when this has been encouraged by their parents or teachers*.

But, step out of 'what the family or society thinks', abandon the 'oughts and shoulds' and embrace the 'new', and a whole new vista of opportunity opens up. You becomes 'I'.

Grounding yourself

You will never be successful at manifesting if you only have a toehold in incarnation and are an 'airhead': head in the clouds, full of ideas but no practicality. It is essential to ground yourself thoroughly and to be centred in your core before working on the exercises or laying the grids in this book. This can be done through the earthy chakras below your feet, and linking in the knees and belly with the assistance of Flint, Smoky Quartz, Hematite or other grounding stones. (You will find an illustration of all the chakras on page 50.)

Symptoms of ungroundedness

Check out these symptoms. Tick more than three or four and you definitely need to ground yourself!

- Bank account is frequently in the red
- Inability to handle the everyday world
- Mental confusion/inability to concentrate
- Life and home are cluttered
- Eyes are blank: 'no one home'
- Spaced out, vague and unfocused
- Difficulty in motivating yourself
- Leaving everything to the last minute, but not living in the moment
- Always running late
- Dizziness or 'woozy headed'
- Clumsiness and dyspraxia – you often bump into

things
- Appearing to float several inches above the floor
- Sugar craving and a desire for junk food
- Constantly hungry but food doesn't satisfy
- Falling asleep while meditating
- Car or electrical equipment breaks down regularly
- Irritability without due cause
- Insomnia and restless sleep
- Unwanted out-of-body experiences
- Sense of looking down on yourself from above
- Body feels heavy and 'alien'
- Emotional and highly overreactive
- Constantly exhausted
- Great ideas or plans that never come to fruition
- Belching or breaking wind frequently
- Anxiety or unease with no apparent cause
- Displaying the same symptoms as someone you were just with
- Mood changes suddenly when passing a stranger or entering a room

Creating your grounding root

This simple grounding root exercise anchors you to the planet, re-energizes you from the Earth, and allows freedom of movement in order to reach higher or further dimensions of consciousness, to journey inwards or back into the past, and to safely access the Akashic Record. Remember to cleanse and dedicate your crystals before you begin the exercise (see pages 24–28).

Creating your grounding root

- *Cleanse the aura and chakras with Flint and/or Anandalite (if you don't have Anandalite or the other crystals you can use the cards in* The Crystal Wisdom Healing Oracle *pack).*
- *Stand with your feet slightly apart, well balanced on your knees and hips. Feet flat on the floor. Place a Flint, Eye of the Storm (Judy's Jasper), Graphic Smoky Quartz, Hematite, Smoky Quartz, Smoky Elestial Quartz or other grounding stone at your feet.*
- *Picture the earth star chakra about a foot beneath your feet opening like the petals of a water lily.*
- *Place your hands just below your navel (tummy button) with fingertips touching and palms out towards the hips.*
- *Picture roots spreading across your belly, into your hips and then down through your legs and out of your feet to meet in the grounding stone.*
- *The two roots twine together and pass down through the*

earth star and the Gaia gateway, going deep into the Earth. They pass through the outer mantle, down past the solid crust and deep into the molten magma.

- *When the entwined roots have passed through the magma, they reach the big iron crystal ball at the centre of the planet.*
- *The roots hook themselves around this ball, holding you firmly in incarnation and helping you to be grounded in incarnation.*
- *Energy and protection can flow up this root to keep you energized and safe.*
- *Allow the roots to pass up from the earth star through your feet, up your legs and the knee chakras and into your hips. At your hips the roots move across to meet in the base chakra and from there to the sacral and the dantien just below your navel. The energy that flows up from the centre of the Earth can be stored in the dantien.*

Note: Whenever you are in an area of disturbed earth energy or environmental unrest, or a place where you have a traumatic previous life or genealogical connections, protect your earth star and Gaia gateway chakras by visualising a large protective crystal tube all around them. The root will still be able to pass down to the centre of the Earth to bring powerful energy to support you, and the crystal will help to transmute and stabilise the negative energy. A virtual crystal can work equally well when visualised with intent, but placing an actual crystal here intensifies the effect.

Are you really you?

Alienation leads to the perversion of all values.
Erich Fromm

Alienation is a concept that profoundly affects your prosperity. It may be an internal self-alienation – cut off from a true knowing or loving of your Self – or alienation from an outer community. Alienation from yourself means that you don't value yourself, have no sense of self-esteem or knowledge of your true capacities and potential. Alienation from the family or society may lead to one of two things: 'people-pleasing' in an attempt to gain acceptance, which may mean going against one's own true values and path in life. Or, an angry, 'knee-jerk' rejection of the values and support of that family or society, which may mean 'throwing the baby out with the bath water', and which can also lead to going against your true vocation or, unconsciously, punishing yourself by lack of abundance. On the other hand, we've seen that family and society can preprogram you and we'll be going on to look at the effects of karmic imperatives, soul contracts and soulplans, and how to overcome these obstacles to true prosperity in a moment.

But first, ask yourself:

- Is my lifestyle and my work actually my free choice?

- Am I a 'people-pleaser'?
- Do I feel guilty when I do something that upsets my parents or my family?
- Do I live by rules instilled by my family or their perceived position in society?
- Do I feel like a kid again when I go back to my parents – or their memory?
- Do I feel smothered by my family and their expectations and demands of me as an adult?
- Do I fear that my family will abandon me, financially or emotionally?
- Am I enmeshed, confused and pressured into being something I am not?
- Do I live a double life? Is that satisfactory *to me*?
- Are my financial goals governed by what my parents, or society, expects of me?
- Do I have my own boundaries? Am I separate from my family and their demands on me?

If you answer yes, or are not sure about your answers to these questions, you'll find exercises in this book to help you identify exactly how caught up you are in family expectations. And you'll find crystals that will help you free yourself and become autonomous. Always remember that, if you keep on doing what you've been doing – following 'the rules' – you'll get what you always got. Change how you operate, alter the place instead that you are coming from, and life will reflect something very different back to you.

How do you feel about money?

It is not the man who has too little, but the man who craves more, that is poor.

Seneca

Your beliefs around prosperity have an enormous bearing on the amount of money you attract into your life. How you feel about money determines what you do with it, with how and what you spend it on, the pleasure you get out of it, how long it stays with you – or even whether it comes to you in the first place. So often what underpin your feelings are cultural and family mindsets.

How do YOU feel?

First off, notice how you feel about the statement above. How does your body respond? Then ask yourself what you really believe about money. Does money excite and inspire you, or does it feel uncomfortable even thinking about it? Does your body squirm, your mind immediately go into scarcity mode? Does it depress you because you lack money and can't see that you'll ever have any? Do you spend hours in fruitless imaginings based around 'when I win the lottery', and so on? Do you hoard money 'just in case' and live a fundamentally impoverished life in the meantime?

For some people money is one asset among many, something one either has or doesn't have but it's not particularly important. For other people, and indeed some cultures, money is all there is. It's how they measure status. It's the basis of their self-worth and how they assess themselves against other people. If they lose their money, they feel like they've lost everything. Let's look at why that might be.

Have you ever been told that life is a struggle, you have to work hard for what you get, the economy is failing so it's all downhill from here and you'll never be able to afford that to which you aspire? Was there a message in your childhood that rich people are greedy and there is virtue in poverty, or the opposite: 'easy come, easy go, there's always tomorrow'? Deep down inside do you believe that the world owes you a living, that you have to be practical, there's no room for dreams; or that there isn't enough to go round, that someone has to suffer or do the dirty jobs in life, or that the only job worth having is one with security and 'prospects'? Were you taught that the spiritual path and money don't go together, or that 'people like us don't have jobs like that'? Were you told that it's selfish to want things for yourself and that money is the root of all evil?

Many of us were unknowingly programmed with toxic thoughts like these from a young age and many of those thoughts become excuses or substitutes for generating abundance. If you believe any of the above statements you are unlikely to feel inwardly prosperous or to have a healthy attitude towards money. Toxic programming such as this leads to poverty, not prosperity, consciousness.

If someone gave me a million pounds right now, what I would do with it? Would I instantly pay off the mortgage, buy a house, put it in the bank for a rainy day, go out and blow the lot? Or, as someone I knew said: "Give it to the charity who drill water wells for Africa."

Take a few minutes to write down everything that comes to mind. It could tell you a great deal about what you really feel and believe about money.

The woman who responded to that question with 'Give it to Water Aid' was living an outwardly prosperous middle class life in a beautiful house, but her husband was struggling to pay the mortgage despite his high salary. She dressed in hand-me-downs 'to save money'. It was as though by behaving – and looking – as if they were poor and struggling, they 'paid' for living in the beautiful home and that somehow made it acceptable.

When she examined her response, she realised that she'd been taught in childhood that charity was what mattered. Her parents' view was that if you had 'spare' money you should give it to the poor and needy. It wasn't something to be enjoyed, nor to provide more than the basic necessities in your life. A classic case of poverty consciousness. Even though her parents were comfortably off, they lived a miserly life and, paradoxically, saved hard 'just in case'. As so often happens, the 'just in case' materialised and all their money went on care in their old age so there was nothing for the daughter to inherit.

With the assistance of Green Calcite, the woman began to ask herself whether this was really how she felt. She soon realised that, although she'd been saying that the universe was abundant and that all would be well, *she hadn't behaved like that*. She had unconsciously lived out her parents' pattern. So, she changed her attitude to money. There wasn't any more money in her life, but she felt enriched by what she had. Somehow, there was always enough.

To ask yourself more questions about your attitude to money, turn to pages 93–96.

What do you value?

Until you value yourself, you can't expect anyone else to do so.
John Frederick Demartini

You are your greatest asset. So, do you value yourself? Do you give yourself the love, respect, validation and compassion that you deserve? Do you feel enriched by knowing yourself in all your complexity and beauty? Do you like being you? And do you value other things that lack monetary worth but which enrich your life? What you value has a powerful effect on how you spend your life. Do you value friendship and the company of like-minded people, the joy of sharing time with those you love?

You probably value what you were brought up to believe was valuable and you are rich indeed if you were taught to value not only your true self but also nature and beauty and joy. If you weren't, there's no time like the present to take a look at all the wondrous things around you.

'The poor' aren't just financially deprived. They often lack communication skills, have low expectations and a distorted sense of their own worth – *or other people do on their behalf*. What they do value may be money-based or anything that buys a few moments of forgetfulness. What is rare is a sense of well-being. To get out of a poverty trap a fundamental change in values is needed –

and a change in focus. Watching a magnificent sunset is a deeply enriching experience as are a few moments of silent communication, or contributing to society. It all depends on what you value. Simply taking time to be yourself can be the most enriching thing of all. So, ask yourself what you really value and how much time you give to the things that truly matter in your life:

- *Write down ten people you admire and why you admire them, the qualities that give them value in your eyes. Do you recognise that quality in yourself.*
- *Make a list of the twenty things you value most in life. How many of these are free? Did your list include yourself?*

How much value do you give to your time?

Let your life lightly dance on the edges of Time like dew on the tip of a leaf.
Rabindranath Tagore

Time can be a precious commodity in these pressured times. If you are overburdening yourself with work, running to stand still, then ask yourself:

- How much of my time is filled with things I value and how much with things that have to be done to make money?
- Could I downshift without losing my sense of worth? (If not, see pages 129–142.)
- Would a smaller house, less material goods and more time spent playing with my children, being with my lover, or simply walking the dog be beneficial?
- Could I find time to meditate for five minutes each day?
- Could I delegate or drop many of the things that make me feel so pressured?
- Could I find time to be mindful of all the things around me that could give me joy if only I noticed them?
- Could I donate a portion of my time to help

others?

- What, in how I spend my time, do I value most of all?

People who take time out of their day for quiet communion with themselves or their god – in other words for meditation or prayer – have an inner resource of deep peace and contentment that serves them well on their journey through life. The Dalai Lama says that, if he is exceptionally busy, he gets up even earlier to fit in an extra hour's meditation. If you're short of time, meditation can be fitted into your journey to work (assuming you're not driving), or done last thing at night as a quiet wind-down before bed. (See my *Crystal Mindfulness*.) You don't have to sit still though. Try a fifteen-minute walking mindfulness meditation in your lunch hour in which you simply notice, and have gratitude for, all the little things around you. The laughter of a child at play, the beauty of a bird, the shape of a cloud, the colour of the sky or the lusciousness of a flower. The sounds, the smells and the rich variety of people you pass by. Smile as you do so.

Valuing work

There are people who feel that they have to apologise for what they do, for the job that they have found themselves stuck in, or indeed for the lack of a job. It adds immeasurably to your sense of worth if what you value is the contribution you make to society and to your own well-being through working.

It has always been obvious to me when in Egypt, whether in a hotel or on board a Nile cruise ship, that the staff love their work. Hospitality is valued. They truly want you to enjoy your stay. They are taught, in hotel school, the value of what they do and how to do it well. Their face lights up when they see your delighted reaction to the creations they have made out of towels and bits and pieces. But, it has, of course, long been a tenet of that country that you offer hospitality to a stranger. I've had many a cup of mint tea in a house with a mud floor and very few possessions. But the animated conversation and wide-smiling pride of the host created enormous joy in drinking that cup. I felt truly blessed.

Questions to ponder

- Do I value myself? Am I my most potent and valuable asset?
- Do I take time out to do the things I enjoy simply for the pleasure?
- If not, why not?

What makes you wealthy?

Doing what you love is the cornerstone of having abundance in your life.
Wayne Dyer

Being who you intrinsically are, rather than who or what you – or anyone else – think you should be or become is crucial if you are to value yourself and live an enriched life. Self-esteem, self-respect and self-worth are the basics of your inner wealth. Your self-esteem should not rest on how much money you have in the bank or in what you own or what other people think of you, but in who you are as a person. Living in alignment with your deepest beliefs makes you wealthy.

Low self-esteem is indicated by a need for external validation, the good opinion of others, status symbols and trappings of success: fast car, big house, social acceptance and trophy wife or husband or its equivalent. It's shown by a desperate need to prove yourself, or an insatiable greed for approval and a desire to win at all costs. It's signalled by deep dissatisfaction with yourself, constantly thinking you need to be 'better', and a tendency to people-please or adjust your views to reflect those of people you consider to be more important than yourself. It's about an unconscious lack within yourself that drives you to seek in another what is missing in yourself instead of recognising it within your self.

The biggest barrier to prosperity is that, in many

cultures, we are taught to value ourselves for what we achieve in the external world or how we fit into the idea someone else has of us. This is often accompanied by the view that the individual must subsume his or her needs for the good of the whole. But this is not so! Abundance is all about appreciating and valuing yourself *exactly as you are right now*. Having an unshakeable sense of your own inner worth is one of the richest resources you have. So how do you get it?

> *Start being you.*
> *The you who is here right now.*
> *Manifest who you truly are.*

Build up your sense of worth a step at a time. Each time you waver, tell yourself you have equal value to everyone else. It's not about what you do but rather about who you are. Nevertheless, what you achieve can be a foundation for self-worth. Make a point of noticing all the little things you do – and set sensible goals that you can easily achieve rather than shooting for the moon. Each time you achieve something, each task that you fulfil, each goal you reach successfully, each good day you have, pat yourself on the back. Give yourself a treat – treats do not need to centre around money. Don't beat yourself up for not doing more. Respect yourself for what you have achieved rather than for what you have not yet done. Be as kind and compassionate to yourself as you'd like other people to be to you.

- *Write down all your qualities, everything you have to offer, everything on which your true worth is based. Start each sentence with: "I am valuable because........." and remember to add to the list each time you notice something else for which you have value.*

This list will no doubt change and develop over time, and tracking what you feel is important enough to list teaches you a great deal about yourself and what you value in yourself. (If you are in any doubt about what you value, turn back to pages 82–83.)

Paradoxically, being able to generously share or give away what you have makes you wealthy. In remote places, people who have little in the material sense share what they have. They show kindness to a stranger. They offer an opportunity to show compassion and kindness in return. Giving our time and our listening skills is just as valuable if not more so as giving a donation. A smile and a word of encouragement cost nothing but could change a life.

Right livelihood has long been one of the principles of the spiritual path, as has service to humanity. If you are true to yourself and you live and work and have your being in accordance with what you value, then you are wealthy indeed. Score yourself on the following wealth points on a scale of 1 to 10.

Wealth points:

- Self-respect: a sense of your own worth and value based on 'who I am', not 'what I do'.
- Self-esteem: a sense of acceptance of yourself and your having achieved a goal no matter how small.
- Self-worth: a sense of integrity and congruence, being aligned with your self and honouring your truth.
- Inner peace (see pages 184–185).

How well did you do? Return to this page from time to time and score yourself as you work with the book.

The Attractor Factor

Like attracts like.
(Unknown source)

Ask yourself whether you an attractor or a repeller? Do you attract good fortune or push it away? Do you let in the good stuff or shut off the flow? The choice is yours. The biggest contribution you can make right now to your ability to attract prosperity is to monitor your thoughts and look at what you believe deep down inside yourself because this is what creates your world.

"Why would anyone push good fortune away?" you may ask. But we all do it from time to time, simply by the way we think and what we believe. If your core beliefs are negative, or if they deny what you really want, change them! Remember that like attracts like and opposites repel. If you have a constant litany of negative thoughts running through your head, transform it. Focus on feeling enriched and believe that you create what you need. Start attracting all the good things of life to you, not just money. By releasing our self-limiting beliefs, leaving behind the conditioning of childhood and culture, we align to a totally different energetic blueprint. What you talk about, and put your thoughts on, manifests.

The desire for money or for more, more, more rules many people's lives. As a result it never feels like there is enough. They never feel satisfied. All the energy goes into accumulation and greed to feed that insatiable itch for more. If the purpose of life is financial success and that eludes you, what then? Life is empty, or appears that way. And when you feel barren, what you attract to yourself is even more barrenness to bolster that feeling of there not being enough. If you start to feel gratitude for what you have rather than demanding 'more!' you create a space in which more manifests. Don't limit what you attract, add: "this or something better".

And remember that it may not be quite as you visualise. What you ask for may manifest in a completely different way because that is what you need to fully enrich your life.

Take a small step now: Create an altar – not an altar to money but rather a sacred space in which prosperity manifests in your life. Put crystals, pictures and items that symbolise not only what you want to attract into your life but all the good things that already enrich your life for which you are thankful. Place at least three crystals to magnify the energy.

Clarifying what you really want

Knowing what we really want is crucial for prosperity. When we first start to ask the universe for things, or to manifest our inner riches, we tend to be confused about what it is we actually want because we aren't used to focusing on exactly what 'it' is. What we think we want can so easily be confused by other, deeper needs. Getting to the bottom of what you really want takes a bit of digging, but is worth it.

Do you really want a big, expensive car that would make you feel good because you'd score a point over all those people who thought you were a loser, for instance? Are you trying to bolster your self-image and it's not about asking for a car at all? In that case, look deeper into what you really want and work on finding that. Or do you want a serviceable, comfortable car that gets you where you want to go with the minimum of fuss and maximum efficiency? Simply ask for a car. It is questions like these that have to be addressed before you manifest prosperity. Otherwise, not only do mixed messages get sent out but you are never satisfied when you get what you ask for because it won't be what you really wanted in the first place.

Ask yourself what you want right at this moment. What would make you feel good? If the answer is a piece of chocolate, ask yourself why. Are you seeking the scrumptious taste and amazing sensation as it melts on your tongue and trickles down your throat? Do you actually relish each moment it's in your mouth or do you stuff it down so fast you don't taste it? If the scrumptiousness is what you're after, you're pretty clear on what you want. But if you're stuffing it down then you're probably doing just that: stuffing it down on top of something that threatens to make you feel poor, uncomfortable, somehow lacking, depressed. Maybe it's an endorphin hit you're seeking? Or, perhaps, a comfort blanket to stop unhappy feelings rising up and taking over. If so, it won't matter how many bars of chocolate you consume, you won't actually feel any better. Sometimes what you really need is a hug or someone to listen and say, "Yes, I know how you feel. It's OK to feel like that."

So, once you've had the 'I want' thought, take a moment to clarify exactly what it is you really want. Write your initial want down and keep asking yourself:

- *Is this what I truly want or it is something else?*
- *What does this want rest on?*
- *What would satisfy my deepest need?*
- *What would truly enrich me?*

Once you've established what lies beneath what you think you *want*, then you clearly ask for what you *need*. Nevertheless, even when you've clarified what you're asking for, other things may get in the way. Ask yourself whether you were ever told:

- "I want doesn't get."
- It's wrong/bad/selfish to want things for yourself.
- It's no good wanting.
- No good ever comes of wanting things like that.

What else were you told? Take a few moments to contemplate the kind of messages you were given in childhood or have picked up since. Turn these around into positive statements, in the moment, not the future statements, such as "All my needs are met", "I have what I need", "I wish only good for myself" and so on.

Giving yourself what you want

Go back to a moment in childhood when you really, really, really wanted something. Close your eyes and picture yourself there, feel all the feelings associated with that moment, how intense that sense of wanting was.

- Did you get it?
- How did that make you feel?

If you didn't get what you wanted, change the picture now:

- *Hold an appropriate crystal. Close your eyes again and visualise your younger self being given exactly what you asked for. Feel the excitement, the joy, the satisfaction of being given exactly what you wanted. Remember that you can give yourself that feeling at any moment by giving yourself what you need. You do not have to rely on other people to fulfil your needs. Gift yourself joy.*

Was it satisfying?

How long did the satisfaction last? If it was fleeting it could indicate that there was a deeper need underlying that childish want. Also note how emotionally attached you were to the outcome. Children are usually strongly attached to outcomes. They think their world will end if they don't get what they want. As an adult, can you feel that intensity of wanting and yet maintain a sense of detachment from the outcome? It is extremely productive when you can be dispassionate about a result.

Ask with clarity

Finally, once you know exactly what you want, ask for it clearly and unambiguously in as short a sentence as possible. Practise until you refine your wants into succinct needs.

Holding a clear intent

Before you frame your intention or magnetise a crystal, read pages 14–17. Clarity is essential if you are to manifest prosperity in all its guises.

Starring in your own soap opera:
The Karpman Triangle

Karpman situations can be glamorous and seductive, they can be dramatic and exciting, which is why some people become addicted to them, and find it hard to kick the habit, even when they are suffering.
Brian Parsons

So often a great part of our prosperity-blocking comes from repeating ingrained soul dramas over and over again. Soul dramas are patterns that are carried over many lifetimes, often on a grand scale, but they play themselves out in small day-to-day interactions in the current life – especially but certainly not limited to within the family. Whenever you feel guilty, smothered by your family, angry at others, try to please others or revert to being a child again, you are taking on a role in an ongoing soul saga.

One set of these soul dramas is known as 'the Karpman Triangle' and is of the 'swings and roundabouts variety', stuck on the karmic wheel and going round and round within a loosely connected soul group. Not all members will be in incarnation at the same time but will meet time and again across a cycle of incarnations within a familiar soap opera script. It can have a profound effect on your prosperity.

Members may play out the same role each time, or

experience opposite ends of the cast list. Victim becomes rescuer; rescuer turns persecutor; and back to victim. The victim often switches to persecutor because it gives a – spurious – sense of power. Stepping off that karmic wheel allows for change. But, hidden in the depths of the drama, soul gifts are being developed. Compassion, strength, flexibility, patience, insight. The list is wide. The trick is to know when to step off the wheel, out of the soap opera, cutting loose but taking the soul gifts with you.

The Karpman Triangle can include the 'identified patient syndrome' in which one member of a family, or group, takes on the role of family scapegoat. Illness, poverty, mental instability, addictions (see *Crystal Prescriptions volume 7*), and so on, provide a focus for the, alleged, family concern, overprotection, alienation – and blame. But, when the identified patient moves out of that role, the family is left floundering. They then have to look at their own part in the drama. Face up to their traumas and buried emotions. Identify what they are creating, what they are refusing to look at in their own lives, and how they are perpetrating the role. Few families are that brave.

Crystals are particularly useful for resolving the 'Drama (Karpman) Triangle' of Rescuer-Persecutor-Victim that plays itself out in so many ways in this and other lives. All the zodiac signs are prone to this drama triangle in one form or another, often with one of the roles prominent and the others acting as a hidden agenda underneath. Relationships are a fertile ground for soul dramas. There is a great deal of psychological displacement and projection in such dramatic social games. It is particularly common in families or relationships, and in addictions, where the roles may be fixed or shifting. Inauthentic 'niceness' or 'people-pleasing' often lies at the heart of the triangle on the karmic wheel.

But do remember, it doesn't take three people to play out a Karpman triangle. Nor do we need several lifetimes. We can do it instantaneously in our head.

How to identify a soul drama

- It feels – and looks to an outsider – exactly as though you are starring in a soap opera that is masquerading as 'real life'. Can you identify the soul drama playing out? The 'poor me', the 'bad you', the 'let me save you', or 'it's all your fault', the 'identified patient' syndrome?
- You enter a new relationship, but quickly recognise an old pattern repeating itself. Addiction in all its forms, abuse, domination, 'master/mistress-slave', and so on (the victim/rescuer or persecutor role).
- You constantly ask, "Why is this happening to me?" (The victim/martyr or scapegoat.)
- You say, "I want compensation for that" (the victim). Or, "You'll pay for that" (persecutor).
- You find yourself saying, "That person will get what's coming to them." (The persecutor.)

- Your vocabulary consists of words like, "ought/should/do as I say/it's only right" (the rescuer or controlling persecutor).
- You believe that "if people did what I said they'd be happier" (rescuer/persecutor).
- You 'do a geographical', moving across the country only to encounter the same old same old.
- The same characters turn up in different guises.
- Familiar 'Family stuff' keeps on playing out. Especially in later relationships.
- You are pulled back by old soul contracts, outdated promises, a feeling of 'owing' something/someone.
- Life is not going the way you hoped it would.
- Someone in the family is constantly ill, either at a physical, mental or psychosomatic level. Taking on the pain of the family and, yet, is often blamed for the family's ills (the scapegoat).
- There are addiction issues in the family.
- Your financial situation reflects one of the Karpman roles.

The Roles

The three basic 'Karpman roles' are those of Rescuer (Saviour), Persecutor (Controller), Victim (Martyr/ Scapegoat). They play themselves out over many lifetimes and may lock people together in outdated soul contracts or promises that have carried over inappropriately. Having promised to look after someone or tried to control them, the rescuer role may lead to anger that the person hasn't done 'what they should have' even though the other person may be unaware of the expectation. This then turns into the persecutor role. Or, they may become someone who looks for recompense/reparation, playing into the victim or the persecutor. Each role has its specific – and allied – emotion.

The Triangle and its underlying emotions:

Fear   Anger

Sadness

The Victim role

The victim feels helpless and powerless. They are incapable of making autonomous decisions, or setting a goal, as they are dependent on the goodwill and approval of others. 'People-pleasing' is common. Although, in actual fact, the victim role is an innately selfish one. The goal of the victim is to seek out a rescuer to support their 'hard-done-by' position in life. They take no responsibility for their life, actions or situation. The 'victim' role is resistant to solution finding and problem resolving. It's often characterized by sentences that start with "yes but...", and is peppered with negatives such as can't/won't/don't/couldn't possibly; always blaming someone or something else as to why.

The victim's almost inevitable chronic shortage of money means that someone has to take care of them – although, a wealthy 'victim' may use their money to ensure that they are always cared for. Almost inevitably, handing over the reins to a financial or other adviser to make decisions that may result in financial collapse. So the other person can then be blamed for 'everything going wrong'. The victim needs a persecutor so that rescuers can align themselves with the victim's perceived persecution and/or weakness. Victim-rescuers are frequently codependent on each other. The victim appears to put everyone else first, but may be innately selfish when playing out the victim role, unconsciously saying, "Actually it's really all about me."

The victim role includes the scapegoat and the

'identified patient' who takes on the family's ills, or the family carer who makes the 'burden' of the welfare, happiness or emotional comfort of the whole family – or a partner or someone other – uniquely their own.

As soon as you think about what people are doing *to* you, or what you are being *'forced'* to take on or the position you are *put in*, you are in victim mode. When you look to others to do it *for* you, you are in victim mode. If you feel guilty about upsetting your parents, family, partner or friends, you are in victim mode. If you seek compensation or reparation/retribution, you are in victim mode. Although, in the case of retribution, this crosses over into the persecutor. Variations on the victim theme are martyrdom and being scapegoated – made the cause of all that is bad in a situation or a family.

The victim says:

"Poor me."

"I don't deserve…"

"I can't help/it's not my fault."

"I can't make a decision without advice."

"I'll never get what I deserve."

"No one understands me."

"This always happens to me."

"But I'm such a caring/generous/giving person."

"I must have been a really bad person in a former life."

"What have I done to deserve this?"

"They'll pay for this."

"I deserve compensation."

"I never asked for this/didn't ask to be born."

"The world is against me." (Victim)

Or, alternatively, "It's all my fault I deserve to be punished." (Martyr)

"No matter what I still love you and will never leave you no matter what you do."

"Walk all over me, it's OK."

"I can't help it, it's my karma."

"I have to be of service no matter what the cost to me."

"After all I've done for you." (Although this spills into the Persecutor too.)

and believes:

"It's not my fault." (This also spills into the persecutor.)

"I should not be heard and, preferably, not seen either."

"I am helpless and have no power."

"Anger is a negative emotion that should never be expressed."

The sadness: I'm not good enough, I have no intrinsic worth.

The Rescuer role

The rescuer often feels inadequate. The rescuer is someone, often in the helping field, who takes on an altruistic role to make them feel better about themselves. "I must be a good person because I'm doing this." Or, to make other people believe they are a good, unselfish person. Their belief about themselves involves a 'care-giver-identity' that projects on to others, thus avoiding working out their own issues.

A rescuer is overly-responsible for other people, but not their own self. They make a decision *for* someone else as they do not believe the other person is capable – thus bolstering their own sense of (in)adequacy. They often – unconsciously or consciously – use money as a means of manipulation, power-over and control. They endure poverty in order to give to others – often, but not necessarily, family members.

As soon as you think about what other people need and put your own needs and happiness aside in pursuit of that goal, you are in rescuer mode. Whenever you rush to assist without thinking it through first, you are in rescuer mode.

The rescuer says:

"Poor you."

"I'll save you no matter how long it takes" – which can carry through many lives.

"I'll always be there for you" – which can carry through several lives.

"How can I help?"

"I am responsible for everyone else's happiness and well-being."

"I have to make reparation/restitution."

"I don't have issues. I'm here to help everyone else."

"I'll do that for you."

"He/she has so much potential I have to stick around to help."

"He/she can't do it without me."

"It will go to pot without me."

"If I left/threw him (her) out, I'd be responsible for what happened next."

And believes:

"I can save the world."

"Without me, s/he'd be nothing."

"They are useless without me."

"It's my job in life to be a doormat." (Which may cross into the martyr role.)

The Fear: If I'm not needed, I don't exist.

The Persecutor role

Persecutors are angry people, though they rarely acknowledge that. They often feel hard-done-by and inferior and so, consciously or subconsciously, seek to control their environment and the people around them to make themselves feel more adequate. They tell other people what their decision, or course of action, *should* be. Persecution can arise out of apparent weakness or helplessness – which in itself is a form of manipulation. But, equally, it may take the form of overseeing a victim's

– or society's – behaviour. Blame is the name of the game. It is a subtle or overt form of control.

Persecutors cannot tolerate a different viewpoint or an alternative lifestyle choice to their own. 'Benign' persecutors give criticism, or instructions, disguised as advice. They may say, "This was my experience, this is how *I* did it...", implying that, if you do not do the same, you are 'wrong' or 'bad'. Overt persecutors simply bark out criticism or orders. As with the victim, they take no ultimate responsibility for their own actions, claiming to be "only following the rules". Often doing so "for your own good", or that of society or the family.

It is never the fault of the persecutor, or anything to do with their own attitude to life. There is always someone else to blame. A persecutor knows and exploits every little weakness and insecurity in another person and highlights every 'flaw' as a way of staying in control. The persecutor consciously uses money as a means of manipulation, power-over and authority. If anything goes wrong financially, it is the fault of the adviser who "wasn't good enough". Or the company/investment that failed.

As soon as you think that what people are doing is wrong, or that there is a better way, you are in persecutor mode. The persecutor-role may include the saboteur and the critic in addition to the control freak and the thought police.

The persecutor says:

"Bad you."

"It's your fault. You got me/yourself into this."

"It's nothing to do with me, it's all you."

"If you weren't so bad this would never have happened."

"If it wasn't for you, I could…"

"If I were you, I'd…"

"I've found that…"

"You're not good enough."

"After all I've done for you."

"You are so ungrateful."

"You are different, therefore you are bad."

"You need to change."

"Stay in line."

"Do what I say or else."

"You'll get what's coming to you."

And believes:

"I have to keep control."

"Without me there would be chaos."

"I know best."

"People must be punished."

The anger: Powerlessness. Envy. Jealousy.

Karpman Triangle exercise

This exercise is about accepting the underlying feeling of each role, so that you understand and recognise it, and then let it go. You will need to allow your intuition, or dowse, to tell you which crystal will work for you *(see the A–Z Directory)*. There is no one 'right way', no 'this will work for everyone'. Don't be afraid to experiment and see which one(s) facilitate release for you.

Note: It is really useful to do this exercise within a support group. The support group hold a safe space and the crystals appropriate for each corner of the triangle. They do not intervene, suggest or acknowledge unless specifically asked for one of the crystals or how standing in that position makes them feel. You may want to dialogue with another role to clarify matters. If so, ask which member of the support group can assist. Or, move back and forth between the two positions on the triangle and listen to yourself. The process should not be interrupted once begun. Offering an opinion immediately puts a support group member into one of the positions on the triangle. Although a support group member may ask the question, "How does that role play out in your life…" which does not necessarily have to be answered aloud.

- *Lay out a triangle on the floor – with an appropriate crystal on the corners.*

- Stand at each point and read through the statements for that role, and see how you feel about it. Honour and accept them as below.

Standing in the victim position: Ask yourself where life seems to be unfair, where you apparently have no control, where other people treat you badly. Place the crystal over your heart seed chakra and ask, what is the sadness hidden deep inside you? Honour that feeling and let it go. Forgive yourself for being vulnerable. [Support group to stand by placidly. Don't intervene even to offer tissues – unless requested. If someone rushes to assist, they are in rescuer mode.]

Standing in the rescuer position: Ask yourself where you take responsibility for someone else's happiness and well-being to the detriment of your own. Who do you feel responsible for? Why? Is that realistic? Do you need to tie-cut or renegotiate a soul contract? What is your deepest fear? Share your secret fear with your support group. Show them who you really are.

Standing in the persecutor position: There is only you. No one else. No one to blame or judge. Don't speak; go deep down into your base chakra and let the anger rise up. Accept it. Take responsibility. Honour it. Channel it up through the sacral to the dantien below your navel. Store the power there. Stand proud and tall with Thulite or one of the other crystals (see below or the A–Z Directory) on your dantien. How can you use this power wisely? How can you assert your Self? [Support group step back and hold a safe space, do not *intervene; honour and acknowledge.]*

- *Which role feels most comfortable?*
- *Which one least?*
- *Then stand in the middle. How does that feel? Balanced??? Are you pulled towards a particular direction?*
- *Then deliberately step out and stand outside the triangle. How does that feel?*
- *Consider your experience. Was there a soul gift hidden at the heart?*

Karpman Antidote Crystals: Thulite (Pink Zoisite), Morganite or Rhodochrosite. Green Dioptase or Chrome Diopside or Green Zoisite or Moss Agate. Sugilite or Charoite, and see the A–Z directory. *Chakra:* Heart seed, base, sacral, heart, throat.

Extending the exercise

Now that you are familiar with the roles, think about your financial situation and your intentions for the future. Note which roles you take on in your life before stepping into the centre:

- *Select one of your financial issues.*
- *Stand in each position on the triangle in turn and feel how/if you could bring that issue to a successful outcome from that role.*
- *Listen to the voices speaking to you in that position.*

What do the voices say?

- *If a voice says anything useful, make a mental note.*
- *If a voice says something that is counterproductive make a note to clear that voice as soon as possible.*
- *Move on to the next positions, repeating the exercise.*
- *Ask yourself which position was the most helpful and which the most unhelpful.*
- *Identify any consistent theme that comes up from the feelings and voices.*
- *Now step into the middle, holding your crystals, and see if the voices balance themselves out.*
- *If you have identified non-helpful voices or feelings, switch them off now (see A–Z Directory for crystals to assist).*

Repeat the exercise for an intention you have for the future. Repeat until you are making decisions from your own autonomous self.

Step out of the triangle altogether before undertaking any of the rituals or layouts in this book.

Soul planning, vows and contracts

[Note: This section has been extracted from my Book of Why.*]*

So often, it is your own soul that is tripping you up. One of the surprising places to find traps that may keep you mired in a poverty trap or the unfulfilled zone is your own Self and its ingrained beliefs, attitudes and intentions. The soul contracts, imperatives, plans, vows and promises that you made in other lives, or between lives, may actually be detrimental *because things have moved on.* Either during the present lifetime, or they were past-their-sell-by date when you incarnated but you hadn't freed yourself from them.

An obvious example of these is the 'poverty, chastity and obedience' vows that *religieuse* make – the monk or nun, not the pastry! Although, the pastry is a good example of how precariously a small, seemingly independent unit balances on a larger foundation. With, in this case, soft squishy comforting cream as a filling. Topped with dark chocolate. Decadent and yummy. Great for some people but, if you have diabetes for instance, lethal for others. As are soul contracts, there is always a 'receiver' who benefits, but the 'giver' does not always do so unless it has been well thought out in advance. So often, such things are merely a carryover from the past.

Your soul's plan: The planning meeting

Under regression, most people who are in the interlife considering their options for the next incarnation visit what I call the planning department. They meet with their higher self, members of their soul group, guides and other advisers and are shown what they have already learned, or failed to learn, in other lives.

So, for instance, some who have been greedy, misusing power and abusing others in order to become wealthy, may, in the interlife, recognise that and want to make reparation. They may choose a life of service, giving back to others. Or, they may, consciously or unconsciously, create a life of lack and loss. Losing whatever money they do have. But the important thing to recognise is that, once that pattern or 'reason' has been identified and the lesson learned, the plan can be changed. It is not set in concrete for the whole incarnation.

The planning meeting frequently presents just like a board meeting with people sitting around a table with audio visual/multimedia equipment ready to review the past and explore possibilities for the future. Discussions are held with those with whom we intend to incarnate once again. If a soul needs to learn a hard lesson or to immerse itself in a particular ambience, mistaken beliefs or toxic emotional states, for the sake of understanding or reframing, then this is when someone from the soul group may volunteer to provide the difficult circumstances which will allow us to develop insight.

A 'resonance frequency', in other words a similar and familiar vibration, may have been set up over several lives within a soul group who all had roles in the soul drama that unfolded, and this may draw a soul group back together, willingly or otherwise, so that the saga can be reworked or framed. If the soul group is conscious and aware of the pattern, then this will be discussed at the planning meeting, but if it is not aware, then the 'resonance frequency' will act like an imperative soul overlay pulling the participants together to re-enact the story once again. Which gives an opportunity to change it. If one soul has become conscious of the saga, this may be enough to break the pattern – provided awareness is retained or reactivated during the current life.

So, at the 'planning meeting', mentors help the soul to assess what progress it has made, to identify the conditions needed for new growth and any reparation or restitution that may be required, and to find appropriate parents to provide the genetic and cultural inheritance, emotional ambience and environmental influences needed for the new incarnation or to create a completely new script, one that is created to serve another in their growth (see *The Book of Why*).

Exercise: Attending your planning meeting
This exercise uses visual imagery but you don't have to

actually 'see' anything to access your soulplan. Some people are clairauditory rather than visual – that is they *hear* or *sense* a voice telling them the information. Other people 'just get a sense' or 'know'. Not expecting things to happen a certain way allows your inner knowing to communicate with you in the most appropriate way. However, looking up to the spot above and between your eyebrows ('the third eye') can help images to form, as can deep relaxation and a crystal on the third eye.

Choose a time to do this exercise when you will not be disturbed, turn off the phone and find a comfortable place to sit or lie. You may find it helpful to record the script or have a friend read it to you with appropriate pauses to allow time for the information to surface. If you have images or a way of accessing the information that is different to the script, go with your own *knowing* but be sure to come back fully into your body at the end:

- *Hold your crystal and ask it to assist you in this process.*
- *Close your eyes and breathe gently, setting up a slow, unforced rhythm. Bring your attention deep into yourself and let any thoughts that are not relevant to the answers you seek simply float past and go on their way.*
- *Picture yourself in a sunny meadow, let yourself feel the grass beneath your feet, smell the flowers, feel a gentle breeze on your face. Enjoy this lovely place for a few minutes and then let your feet take you across the*

meadow to a building you can see in the distance.

- *As you open the door to this building, you will see a lift in front of you. Step into this lift and allow the doors to close. You will see a button marked 'the planning department'. Press this button and allow the lift to take you swiftly up to the level you need.*

- *As the doors open, your higher self will be standing waiting to greet you. Spend a few moments greeting your higher self.*

- *Your higher self will then conduct you to the planning meeting and explain things to you if necessary.*

- *Sitting around a large table you will see all the people with whom you intended to incarnate and the guides and helpers who will assist the process.*

- *Take time to look at each person. Listen to what they have to say, the contributions they made to the planning, and check out the role they will have in your life.*

- *Ask your higher self to reveal to you the soulplan you formulated for your present incarnation and to show you the reasons for your choices where appropriate. (If you need to change anything agree this with your higher self.)*

- *Ask also that you be shown outdated and outgrown soul overlays that may trip you up when putting your soulplan into action. Allow these overlays to dissolve or to be reframed into something more positive and appropriate to your current stage of life (see below).*

- *Before you leave, ensure that you clearly know the*

soulplan you are working to and the parts that people are to play. Thank those people for the task they have taken on.

- *Ask too whether you have agreed to specific roles and, if these are no longer appropriate, adjust or reframe (see below).*
- *When you are ready to return, your higher self will take you back to the lift. The doors will be open, waiting for you. If appropriate your higher self will step into the lift with you. Press the button for the ground floor.*
- *When you step out you will be back in the building that leads out on to the meadow. If your higher self has joined you in the lift, ask that it will be available any time you come back to the meadow.*
- *Walk back to the centre of the meadow.*
- *Then breathe a little deeper, move your hands and feet, and open your eyes. Take time to adjust to being back in your physical body. Stand with your feet firmly on the ground, feeling your connection with the Earth.*
- *Have a warm drink and then write down your experience.*

It may sometimes take several sessions to be able to fully experience the planning process and to access your soulplan. If this is so, ask your higher self and your crystals to assist you by sending clues and triggers into your everyday life to remind you.

Soul contracts

Before we're born our soul agrees to a few things. I like to think of them as contracts you didn't really agree to sign, but that you are still bound to. We don't consciously agree to these things but they are chosen by our higher self, our soul, before we incarnate in this lifetime.
Soul Sister article

A soul contract is an agreement usually but not necessarily made willingly in the interlife (the space between lives) especially at the planning meeting. It may be that the incarnating soul agrees to undertake a specific task, in which case a contract has often been made that the higher self will keep the soul on track, or that one soul will interact with another in a specific way. However, it may also be an agreement that is carried over from a previous life or even from a previous interlife which has not been reconsidered or renegotiated before the present incarnation and which is no longer applicable.

Soul contracts can also arise from pacts, promises and vows especially those such as "I'll always love you/look after you/be there for you." Such contracts may be positive and constructive. Or, destructive. Positive soul contracts not completed in one life may be unwittingly carried over to another and become destructive. Sometimes a soul contract appears to end in a destructive event, but may actually be a positive act by a member of a soul group to assist the soul in moving forward. [See my *Book of Why*.]

Soul contracts are most often made with members of your soul group but not inevitably so – and you may well find that members of your soul group are still trying to insist upon a contract being carried out that is no longer relevant to your purpose or appropriate to the life you have mapped out. Contracts that have passed their sell-by date, or which are in direct contradiction to the intention of the present life, lie behind many of the karmic conundrums that people endure as they compel certain behaviours no matter how much the soul may wish to override them. This is why soulplans sometimes fail, despite all the good intentions they embody.

Do you have a soul contract or soul overlay?

- Do you feel you have a purpose that you are not fulfilling?
- Are you sure you've got a soul purpose but don't know what it is?
- Do you have an overwhelming urge to look after someone?
- Do you demand that someone looks after you?
- Does someone demand that you look after them?
- Do you feel you owe someone/the world something?
- Do you think someone/the world owes you something?
- Do you feel there's unfinished business/karma

somewhere in your life?

- Do you feel like there's a hidden agenda?
- Do you feel you're on a mission/have a task to perform etc?
- Are you compulsive about certain things?
- Have you ever said, "It must be karma"?

If you answer yes to more than one or two of the above you most probably have a soul contract operating in your life. The question is, is that contract personal or does it involve someone else – and is it still relevant?

Exercise: ascertaining your soul contracts

In accessing your soulplan for the present life (page 127) you may come across several soul contracts but there may well be more. This visualisation uses the same framework as attending the planning meeting, but if you have not yet done this, please familiarise yourself with the preparation instructions on page 116.

- *Hold one of the soul contract crystals (see page 266) and ask it to help you access your contracts.*
- *Close your eyes and breathe gently, setting up a slow, unforced rhythm. Bring your attention deep into yourself and let any thoughts that are not relevant to the answers you seek simply float past and go on their way.*
- *Picture yourself in a sunny meadow, let yourself feel the grass beneath your feet, smell the flowers, feel a gentle breeze on your face. Enjoy this lovely place for a few*

minutes and then let your feet take you across the meadow to a building you can see in the distance.

- *As you open the door to this building, you will see a lift in front of you. Step into this lift and allow the doors to close. You will see a button marked 'contracts department'. Press this button and allow the lift to take you swiftly up to the level you need.*

- *As the doors open, your higher self will be standing waiting to greet you. Spend a few moments greeting your higher self.*

- *Your higher self will then conduct you to the contracts department to show you the relevant soul contracts you have and explain things to you if necessary. The contracts may be presented in written or pictorial form. Study them and make sure that you fully understand all that they entail. If the contract is still relevant and appropriate for the current life, hand if back to your higher self. [If not, see the instructions below.]*

- *Ask also that you be shown outdated and outgrown soul contracts that have passed their sell-by date and which may trip you up when putting your soulplan into action. Allow these overlays to be torn up or to be reframed into something more positive and appropriate to your current stage of life. [See below.]*

- *Before you leave, ensure that you clearly know the soul contracts you are honouring and the part that you and other people are to play. Ask too whether you have agreed to specific roles and, if these are no longer appropriate, adjust or reframe as appropriate [see below].*

- When you are ready to return, your higher self will take you back to the lift. The doors will be open, waiting for you. If appropriate, your higher self will step into the lift with you. Press the button for the ground floor.
- When you step out you will be back in the building that leads out on to the meadow. If your higher self has joined you in the lift, ask that it will be available any time you come back to the meadow.
- Walk back to the centre of the meadow.
- Then breathe a little deeper, move your hands and feet, and open your eyes. Take time to adjust to being back in your physical body.
- Stand with your feet firmly on the ground, feeling your connection with the Earth. Have a warm drink and then record still relevant contracts. (Do not record past-their-sell-by-date or rescinded contracts.)
- If you need to renegotiate or rescind an outdated or irrelevant contract, do that now.

123

Make a note of your relevant soul contracts, what you contracted to do and with whom you contracted. These can be renegotiated again in the future if necessary.

Exercise: renegotiating soul contracts

If your soul contract is no longer relevant, it can either be reframed into something more appropriate, or let go entirely (see below). Renegotiating can take several forms; you may want to slightly adjust an agreement or completely change it. Working with your own higher self and the higher self of the other person ensures that this goes smoothly, but if the other person's higher self will not cooperate or if your own higher self is insistent on you fulfilling the contract, ask yourself if that is because you are trying to wriggle out of a valid agreement which, while you may not like it, still has relevance. If that is the case, ask how the contract can be fulfilled with grace, ease and forgiveness. Add the following section into the appropriate place in the exercise to ascertain your soul contracts. If you find visualisation challenging, be sure to open your third eye with a third eye crystal and then *act as if*: That is, even if you don't *see* anything, *feel* it as intensely as you can and act as though it is actually happening.

- *Hold your crystal and, if appropriate, choose one to represent the other person.*
- *Ask that the other person's higher self will join you and your higher self in the contracts department.*
- *Discuss with the other person's higher self how you feel about the contract, where you feel it is still relevant and where it is not. Remember to be open to hearing the other point of view.*
- *Then find a way to reframe the conditions set out in the soul contract that will be agreeable and fair to all parties. Once this agreement is reached, have it take the place of the original agreement.*

Write out your renegotiated soul contract and keep it

where you can see it to remind yourself that things have changed.

Tearing up past-their-sell-by-date contracts

There are times when, with the best will in the world, contracts simply cannot be honoured. If a contract was based, for instance, on another soul fulfilling certain intentions or putting a soulplan into action, which you offered to support or which supported you, you can set a time limit on the contract. If the soul has wilfully refused or been unable to make the transition to a new way of being, or has made no effort to put the soulplan into action, you can end the contract without any karma or consequences accruing. Occasionally, both the higher selves concerned may take some convincing of this, in which case unilateral action on your part may be necessary if you are sure that you have done all you can and want the karma of grace (which basically says 'enough is sufficient') to come into operation so that you can move on – although this will not work if you are trying to wriggle out of something that really is in your soul's best interest. Add the following at the appropriate place in ascertaining your soul contracts:

- *In your mind's eye, take the contract and tear it into small pieces. Place the pieces into a fireproof dish and set them alight.*
- *As the paper smokes and burns, let forgiveness and thanks go the other person but set them and yourself free*

from the contract.

- *When the fire burns out, the contract is ended.*
- *Ask both higher selves to honour the fact that you have rescinded the contract and to release any agreement made between the two of them regarding the contract.*
- *There is an old occult law that says if you ask three times, the request must be honoured and the contracts must be rescinded so, if necessary, repeat the process three times and hand the charred dishes to the higher selves, blowing away the ash as you do so.*

If you know what the wording of the contract was, you can write it on a piece of paper and set light to it as a tangible release, remembering to let go with forgiveness as you do so.

Soulplan or ego script?

Your personal Soul Plan is designed to push you beyond the limits of your Ego mind, beyond your fears and empty Ego desires. It will utilise your strengths and enable you to overcome your 'weaknesses'. It will invite you to step outside of the box in order to become the very best version of yourself, the person you were born to be! It has an energy, a drive, powered by the fire of your passion and your deepest heart's desire to make a difference.
Kat Day

When you look at your soulplan and/or contract, do make sure that it really is the soul or higher self's purpose and not the ego that you engage with. Many of us are here to assist this planet and humanity through troubled times of great change and potentiality *but that can be a subtle ego-trap*. Egos may see this as the end of the world, or a time to be lauded as a 'saviour'. Higher selves tend to see it as an opportunity for much needed changes to occur, but the ego can try to take over and give you a heroic mission that is far beyond what you really planned – and it's not always the higher self who communicates even though it may appear to be.

Ego-traps are extremely seductive. Public adulation can turn anyone's head – and pull them away from something they intended to do quietly out of service. If someone or *something* tells you that you are here to save the Earth – especially at great cost to yourself, watch out!

To fulfil such a soul purpose, the emphasis should be on an individual's contribution and the responsibility each takes for their part in creating the whole, not on public recognition or reward.

Section 3

Enriching Your Life

Living an abundant life

Don't go through life, grow through life.
Eric Butterworth

It is our attitude to prosperity that determines how much abundance we enjoy and whether we live a fundamentally enriched life. In this section we look at what true prosperity is, what it means to you and to how to work with it to create a real sense of abundance and well-being now – and how to attract prosperity of all kinds into your life. We will also examine what may be blocking you. Pointing out that there are many ways of being wealthy, we examine what enriches life in addition to money. The following sections are practical and experiential. The tools include visualisations, affirmations, rituals and layouts using prosperity crystals. You will discover your deepest attitude to wealth, and what works best for you and how you personally are going to interact with the magic of crystals. This is a richness you then take into any area of your life.

Prosperity consciousness

We don't change what we are, we change what we think what we are.
Eric Butterworth

Prosperity is a state of mind and a way of well-being. It is more than having money and possessions, although naturally these have their place. Prosperity consciousness is about feeling satisfied and secure with what you have, living an enriching and fulfilling life, sharing life's bounty, feeling gratitude and trusting that the universe provides appropriately for your needs.

If you are struggling with money issues and especially if you feel stuck in a poverty trap, this definition of prosperity may sound like claptrap. As could the statement that, to a large extent, we create what we experience. But think about it. Many people put all their attention on hard times to come, and wonder why those times quickly manifest. Or, bemoan that hard times are here and wonder why they stay. Many carry forward ancestral patterning and beliefs. They feel that the world owes them a living yet do nothing to create a space where prosperity flourishes, or believe they are a victim of circumstances they cannot change. If you have self-respect, you never feel demeaned by a job or what other people think of you.

Think about your own attitude for a moment. Do you believe that prosperity is all about having money and financial success – and that your world will fall apart if you lose a job or don't achieve your monetary ambitions? Some people – and you may be one of them at this moment – fantasize about the difference having unlimited money makes, the happiness it brings, how different life would be. Desire for money literally rules some people's lives. If they have money, they want more, and more, and yet are never satisfied. They count every penny and never take a moment to truly enjoy the fruits of their labour.

Ask yourself, do you judge your worth – and that of others – by the job done, by status or wealth, and feel demeaned if it is not 'good enough', rather than seeing it as a valuable contribution to society? Do you feel you are 'good enough'? Your inner attitude makes an enormous difference. To someone who feels impoverished, the world invariably looks bleak. To someone who feels powerless, it seems that someone else is in control. To someone who has found their inner powerful, miraculous self, anything is possible. Ask yourself, do I feel like a victim of circumstances? If you do, you are unlikely to view your life as fulfilling and will experience an inner poverty rather than a sense of living a rich life.

But it doesn't have to be like this. True prosperity comes from an inner contentment and generosity of spirit that naturally attracts wealth of all kinds. It comes from the richness of friends, a good work-leisure balance and a healthy attitude to money. And it most certainly comes from trusting that we live in an abundant universe. This doesn't mean pretending that everything's OK, or denying that there are problems. We need to be honest with ourselves. Negative feelings can be useful warnings to us – but you don't have to stay entrenched in them or feel them every day. Nor do you have to go into denial of how you are feeling and pretend to be positive. There is a huge difference between being realistically positive when assessing possibilities and adopting an unrealistic Pollyanna approach that takes no account of actualities such as bills piling up. If you continually assert that things *will* go wrong, they inevitably do. But if you look at what could feasibly go wrong and plan a way through to the other side, setting realistic goals and trusting the process, good things manifest.

Throughout this book we've looked at many different manifestations of richness in life and you learn how to tune into these for yourself. We are exploring the attitudes of mind and core beliefs that hold you back, the fears, self-pity and negative self-talk that gets in the way, and you learn how to surrender to the *process* of prosperity. So, be positive.

Grasp an opportunity when it presents itself, no matter how cunningly it is packaged or how much it might look like a disaster. There will be a bright side.

Start with one small step. *Put a Citrine in your purse and then, no matter how small, make a donation to charity or sponsor someone who is undertaking an activity for charity. See it as the start of your abundance.*

How do you find abundance in your life?

Life is just a mirror, and what you see out there, you must first see inside of you.
Wally Amos

Looking within your own self is the secret of finding true abundance: cashing in on your own resources. You have all the riches and resources you need within yourself to create an abundant world. You just need to believe it. And to tap into your inner world you need the power of intention and sufficient impetus to take those first small steps.

It's all very well, you may be saying at this point, but I'm unemployed or in a low-paid job, or I've lost everything or am in danger of doing so, and none of it's my fault. In other words, you may be feeling sorry for yourself rather than having compassion for the place you find yourself in. You are caught in the Karpman Drama Triangle (see page 97). To 'poor me' the world looks bleak and you appear to lack resources and, as a result, you abandon hope. If you don't feel rich, it is all too easy to feel apathetic, powerless and helpless, and it has been shown that apathy equals poverty, despair and hopelessness. This creates a vicious circle that can be broken by the exercises, visualisations, rituals and layouts that follow. As long as your life feels secure and inwardly enriched, you can wait with equanimity for abundance to manifest itself fully.

Take a small step now: Ask yourself, what is your most enriching quality. Go out and share it with someone right now.

What else enriches your life?

Spirituality, joy, nature, arts, crafts, music, sport, culture, friendship, hobbies and community service are all intrinsically rewarding and make life meaningful, giving it passion. Passion is vitality, drive, intention and sheer joy in living, and when you have it, there is no room in your life for doom, gloom or depression. Passion enables you to find the one thing that you shine at, that makes you unique and special. So, passion is a great life enhancer as is creativity. When we create we put something of our own self into what we produce whether it is writing, painting, music or craftwork, and that feels satisfying and good. You'll notice that most of the valuable assets do not necessarily entail spending money although some of them require you to make an effort.

Friendship

If you have friends with whom you share affection, mutual support and laughter, who broadly share your worldview and your values and of whose integrity you are in no doubt, then your life is immensely enriched. These are the kind of friends who bring out the best in you, who make you feel richer for having known them. The friends who stimulate inner resources that you didn't know you had: patience, tolerance and infinite kindness. This is where fun and joy and wonderment lift you up and make you see the world in a different way. But if your so-called friends are needy and constantly drag you down then perhaps you may need to look on friendship from another angle. Are you with them because they make you feel needed – or superior? Many people confuse being needed and being useful with feeling good about themselves because by meeting other people's needs they believe they must be meeting their own. But is this true? There is an enormous difference between supporting a friend when it is appropriate knowing that, in turn, you receive the same support and so the friendship is mutual, to spending endless hours propping up someone who is never there for you. The first one energizes and enriches your life, the second depletes it.

Similarly, if you have a friend who constantly tells you how to improve yourself and your life, you are being disempowered by 'friendship' rather than empowered. Friends who believe in you and in themselves equally enrich your life. A friend who says 'go for it' when you try for that job that seems just out of your league and who helps you practise for the interview is a wonderful gift. As is one who tells you when you are truly out of order and freely forgives you for it. And you, in turn, derive great satisfaction from returning the favour. In other words, friendship is a two-way process, give and take are balanced and the friendship is money in your inner piggy bank. Friendship also makes many of the other inner wealth factors much more fun: sport, art, music, hobbies and so on are much more enjoyable when you have a good friend with you.

Spirituality

Many people find great comfort in religion and may find good companionship through their church, but this is not what spirituality is about. Spirituality means having an inner faith that sustains you and a connection to something greater than you, no matter what name you give to it or indeed whether you name it at all. Daily meditation or ongoing mindfulness that connects you to this 'something greater', and the deep well of peace you experience during meditation, immensely enriches your life and crystals make a perfect focus for meditation.

Service

Being of dispassionate service to others allows you to give something back, to show gratitude for what you have and to extend your connection with your fellow human beings. Being of service is a 'state of being' rather than doing as it comes from a place of infinite compassion *not from need or self-doubt*. It is not the martyrdom or victimhood that so often passes for service. Nor is it true service if you are doing it to make yourself, or others, feel that you have worth and value. True service means doing whatever you are called upon to do with a glad heart and with no thought of recognition or reward. Some of the most potent acts of service are the secret ones that only you know about, performed simply for the joy of giving. A smile is an act of service, as is the price of a cup of tea to a homeless person as long as it's given without judgement or patronage. It is by these small acts that we grow our generosity of spirit and set in motion the prosperity flow.

Endorphins

When you exercise, take a long walk in nature or go for a run, practise yoga, or eat a piece of chocolate you are stimulating natural antidepressants within your body, bringing your own feel-good factor into play. When your body is flooded with endorphins it is impossible to feel impoverished so one of the fastest ways to feel enriched is to take appropriate exercise ideally in nature which is deeply appreciated. Crystals have the same effect. Make time for five to twenty minutes of crystal connection each day. It ensures you always feel good. *(See the Crystal meditation for inner peace page 184.)*

A small step: Ask yourself, "What is the most valuable and enriching thing I could do right now?" Do it!

Gratitude and blessings

Reflect upon your blessings, of which every man has plenty, not on your past misfortunes, of which all men have some.

Charles Dickens

Gratitude is a fundamental part of abundance. Over many religions and thousands of years, people tithed a part of their income or produce to their god. This system worked on a fundamentally sound principle: that of showing gratitude for what the universe had provided or for what you had. It was a way of saying 'thank you'. You'll be surprised at how showing gratitude for what you have, rather than yearning for what you have not, changes how you feel into a deep sense of enrichment. Counting your blessings is another ancient tradition, one that you can fruitfully use in your own life today.

You can also circulate your unused crystals. I once met the wonderful 'Crystal Dave' at one of my book signings. He came up to me and opened his mac. It was lined with poachers' pockets full of crystals. As was his waistcoat. Dave was a gifted and intuitive man who had blown his mind in the sixties, and was in and out of mental institutions as he was prone to flashbacks and mania – which may, of course, have been exacerbated by carrying so many crystals on his person. But, there was a purpose. When not hospitalised, he collected crystals from car boot sales and elsewhere. He never paid more than fifty pence and he had the most incredible collection. He said that when all the pockets were full he knew it would be time to go back into hospital. He filled the crystals with healing intent and gifted them to his fellow patients. When he'd given them all away, he left hospital to replenish his stock. He spoke of this as his life purpose.

Even if you have no spare money for projects, you can donate time or used goods, or put your spare produce outside your gate with a notice 'please help yourself' to keep the cycle of universal beneficence flowing.

Another way of appreciating what you have is to show gratitude and simply say 'thank you' even for the smallest things. Many people like to have a 'gratitude rock'. A crystal placed by the front door, or in some other prominent place, that can be touched when passing. At the same time saying, "Thank you," or some other appropriate sentiment.

'I am blessed'

Counting your blessings helps you to focus on what is good and positive in your life, turning your attention away from any perceived lack. Such blessings are not always the obvious ones.

Take time now to write down twenty things in your life for which you feel blessed. These can be anything from the companionship of good friends to an act of kindness from which you have benefited or anything else that comes to your mind.

Once you have got into the habit of thinking of yourself as being blessed, reiterate it often. Affirm 'I am blessed' and you are.

Questions to ponder

- What is the greatest blessing in my life right now?
- What is the smallest blessing?
- What is my most unexpected blessing?
- What is my most exciting blessing?
- What has turned out to be a blessing that at first I thought was a curse?
- Do I show my gratitude and appreciation for everything that is done for me?
- Do I show my gratitude and appreciation for what I have?
- Am I able to show my gratitude and appreciation for the things that I don't feel are a blessing but which may be part of my soul's learning process?
- Do I tithe my earnings or my time?
- What do I contribute to society?

Section 4

Rituals and Layouts for Specific Outcomes

Getting started

In this section you'll find crystal tools, layouts and rituals to assist in manifesting or supporting your prosperity in specific areas of your life or to cover all your prosperity needs. Simply use your imagination and a little ingenuity to match techniques and crystals for specific purposes. A variety of crystals are always given so choose the one that speaks to you, or to which you have already been attracted and so have the crystal in your collection. Always remember to cleanse and magnetise crystals before use. Having magnetised a crystal, you can wear it, carry it with you, or place it in the wealth corner of your home (see page 145). And do, please, read 'Caring for your crystals' before beginning this section.

The layouts in this section begin with very simple clearing layouts followed by a basic abundance layout. One that can be created in moments. It then moves on to layouts that may require some introspection and thought – and incorporate the insights you have already gained so have your notebook to hand. All are tried and tested.

The Wealth Corner

This is not your get rich quick corner! By enhancing the feng shui wealth, abundance and prosperity area, you will develop a way to gradually accumulate wealth in an honest and safe way. And remember, "If it ain't broke don't fix it!"
www.feng-shui-and-beyond.com

The wealth corner is found in Chinese Feng Shui – an ancient method of bringing energetic harmony into your home. Although not a crystal tool, the bagua below is the perfect guide to placing crystals, grids and altars, or areas in which to carry out rituals for abundance. There are various systems, some based on the compass and others with colour attached, but the easiest way to divide your house up is from the front door. This puts the wealth corner at the far back left-hand corner of the house or a room.

Front door/entrance

Wealth & Prosperity	Fame & Recognition	Relationships
4	9	2
Purple, Blue, Red	Red	Red, White, Pink
Wind	Fire	Earth
Health & Family	Center	Creativity & Children
3	5	7
Green	Yellow	White
Thunder	Unity	Lake
Inner Knowledge	Career	Helpful People & Travel
8	1	6
Turquoise, Blue	Black	Grey, White
Mountain	Water	Heaven

The Bagua

In the bagua parts of the home relate to your business success (the area around your front door) and your fame or personal success (the area on the opposite side of the house to the front door). Scholarly success is found on the left-hand side of the business area with a good family life between it and the wealth corner. The area of success for your children is on the right-hand side between the relationship corner on the far right, and international trade and/or mentors is in the right-hand corner of your front door depending on which system you are following, but there is no reason why it can't be both (see illustration). Each area has an elemental and colour connection although it is not necessary to stick to traditional colours if you use a crystal appropriate to your purpose (*see* The wealth corner crystal, *below*). To attract or enhance success in any of these areas, place suitably magnetised large crystals in the appropriate area.

The wealth corner crystal

Citrine is an ideal stone for the wealth corner. As long as there is no 'sink spot' for the money to flow down, placing a large generator-shaped stone or cluster generates more wealth of all kinds for your home. A sphere here will ensure a smooth in and out flow of resources. If your wealth corner is situated in an area where money flows in and straight out again – a 'sink spot' such as when a bath or cloakroom or drain from a kitchen sink is sited here – a large Citrine geode helps you to preserve your money and to stop you, for instance, flushing your money 'down the pan'.

Feng Shui and crystal prosperity
In addition to the bagua, you can also use Feng Shui, the Chinese system of energy management. It utilises crystals to move energy in a harmonious fashion.

The Feng Shui prosperity stone
Iridescent Ammolite flashes coloured fire and has been dubbed the Feng Shui prosperity stone. It creates, conserves and emanates prosperity on all levels. Each colour represents a specific type of prosperity and can be used to choose crystals to stimulate appropriate areas:

Red: energy and growth
Orange: increased sexual energy and creativity
Green: entrepreneurship and wisdom
Yellow: wealth and intellectual prosperity
Blue: peace and good health
Purple: spiritual well-being and evolution

The effect of crystal shape on Feng Shui

Spheres or balls
Spheres radiate calm and slow down racing currents or chaotic energy, or conversely, speed up stagnant energy. They move energy smoothly around a space and absorb negativity. Balls generate light and harmony. The type of crystal has a specific effect. A large clear Quartz ball in

the main living area neutralises negative emotions and prevents arguments, giving clarity on situations, while a Smoky Quartz sphere grounds energy and defuses tension. A Rose Quartz sphere creates a gently soothing, nurturing energy in a child's room or love into a bedroom, while a Citrine ball alleviates money worries. An Eye of the Storm sphere in the centre of the house diffuses an aura of calm throughout the whole building.

Place your crystal sphere:

- Halfway down a small hallway that has many doors leading off.
- In a long, narrow and dark hallway at the end of the hallway to reflect light back.
- In the centre of a long unbroken wall or hallway – place the sphere as close to the centre as possible.
- On the sill of a window or mirror that is opposite the front door.
- Where a dagger-like energy current strikes a house from an approaching road, crossroads or a corner. Place the crystal in a front window or by the front door to divert the energy.
- Halfway down a set of rooms that open out of each other to slow the rapid energy flow.
- At the top of the stairs if these lead immediately up from the front door.
- In a dark corner or dead end to avoid a build-up of stagnant energy and to draw in light.
- If a road sweeps past a house rushing energy

along with it, place a sphere near to or outside the front door or nearest corner *(see below)*.

- By a cash register to attract good fortune to it.

Diverting an energy arrow

If a road or other energy line heads directly towards your door, place a sphere or large crystal at the point of impact outside the front door to divert or harmonise the arrow.

A house placed here would receive a dagger of fast moving 'negative' energy from two directions where the roads intersect, which crystals placed outside the front of the house or just inside the front door could deflect. Energy could also rush past the house along the major road, taking prosperity with it, and an appropriate crystal to the side of the door would slow it down and harmonise it.

Quick Clearing Grids

If you discover toxic thought patterns, beliefs or ingrained emotional responses during your self-exploration, you can clear the blockage with a simple grid that works on the etheric body before commencing the prosperity layouts. The clearing crystals draw off the toxic pattern, the grounding crystal keeps you anchored in the here and now; and then the 'holding-space' crystal fills the resulting energetic 'hole' with light to allow time for a new, beneficial pattern to be inputted. It is said that Nature abhors a vacuum, and this is very much the case when something toxic has been released from the etheric body and the spaces between the cells in your physical body or chakras. Crystals fill the space with 'light' energy rather than something heavy and anti-abundance. Many crystals, such as Anandalite, Calcite or Brandenberg Amethyst, fulfil both purposes. Alternatively, you can grid your space using one of the layouts from pages 37–46.

Toxic thoughts or beliefs

You will need:
6 clearing toxic thought crystals *(see A-Z Directory)*
1 holding-space crystal *(see A-Z Directory)*
1 grounding crystal *(see A-Z Directory)*

- *Cleanse your crystals.*

- *Place a grounding crystal at your feet and then lie down.*
- *Place a holding-space crystal above your head (point down if it has one).*
- *Place a pair of toxic thought crystals over and above your shoulders (point out if the crystals have one).*
- *Place a pair of crystals level with your ears (point out).*
- *Place a pair halfway between the holding-space crystal and your ears.*
- *Consciously bring to mind the thought that you are releasing. Then let the crystals draw it out while the holding-space crystal inputs light.*
- *State out loud the beneficial thought pattern that replaces the toxic one.*

Toxic emotions

You will need:

2 clearing toxic emotion crystals *(see A-Z Directory)*

1 holding-space crystal *(see A-Z Directory)*

1 grounding crystal *(see A-Z Directory)*

- *Choose an appropriate toxic emotion crystal from the list in the A–Z Directory or use Emerald and Cherry or Strawberry Quartz.*
- *Cleanse your crystals.*
- *Place a grounding crystal at your feet and then lie down.*
- *Place a holding-space crystal over your heart chakra.*

- *Place emotional clearing crystals over your heart seed and higher heart chakras. (Note: if using Emerald and Cherry or Strawberry Quartz check which needs to go above and which below the heart chakra.)*
- *Consciously feel the emotion you are releasing and let the crystals dissolve it.*
- *State out loud the beneficial emotion that will replace it – unconditional love for yourself always works!*

The simplest of layouts

At its heart, a prosperity layout is simply a geometric shape laid out in crystals *with intent*. That intention, in this instance, is to call abundance into your life. This layout only takes moments to create. If your crystals have points, point them in the direction of the centre to draw the energy in. Choose either a simple spiral or the pentangle layout(see 39) and place it in the wealth corner of your home (see page 145) where it will not be disturbed.

You will need: 5 (or more) prosperity crystals. (Citrine or Goldstone would be particularly suitable but see the Prosperity Stones Compendium page 209 and the A–Z Directory.)
Small golden background cloth or card.

The layout:

- *Having cleansed your crystals, hold them in your hand and firmly state your intention that they draw prosperity and abundance to you.*
- *Place the first crystal at the top of the spiral or the pentangle.*
- *If using the pentangle, follow the line down to the right and place the crystal at the point. If making a simple spiral, place the crystal moving towards the centre.*
- *Continue placing the crystals to complete the layout.*
- *Join the points with a wand or the power of your mind.*

If laying the pentangle, remember to go back to the top to close the layout. If laying the spiral, start at the top and then pull the wand, or your mind, up and out from the centre to radiate the energy into your environment.

- *Leave the layout in place undisturbed to do its work.*

Drawing abundance in

The crystals point in the direction of flow. If you wish to draw abundance into yourself, point them towards the centre. A 'keystone' (see page 47) placed in the centre collects the energy for later use, such as keeping in a pocket or leaving in the wealth corner.

The in-depth Abundance Layout

Abundance is about living fully physically, mentally, emotionally and spiritually. Generating and drawing abundance to you entails both mental and emotional focus, opening your mind to the new possibilities that living in the abundant universe opens up for you. This ritual connects you to the spiritual abundance all around and helps you to live abundantly. It builds on the work you have already done to recognise what true abundance is and how it enriches your life.

You will need:
5 cleansed and magnetised prosperity stones (Tiger's Eye, Carnelian, Citrine, Jade, Goldstone or other stones of your choice)
Brightly coloured cloth
Abundance treasure map (see pages 176–177)
1 metre of cord

Preparation: Read through your answers to the questions in Sections 2 and 3. Prepare your abundance treasure map including all the things that you have identified make you feel abundant, not just those related to material wealth. Lay out your cloth and place your abundance treasure map in the centre when you are ready to begin. Hold the intention that this layout helps you to manifest true abundance in your life.

The Abundance Layout:

Choose a place for this layout where you can leave the treasure map (see page 176) undisturbed. The wealth corner of your house (see page 145) is ideal for this layout.

- *Place your treasure map on a brightly coloured cloth.*
- *Starting at the centre of your treasure map, lay a cord spiral out to the edge or, alternatively, simply lay the stones according to the template.*
- *Sit quietly holding your prosperity stones in your hands and reflect on what you have already learned about abundance and true prosperity. Allow yourself to expand and open up to encompass the abundant universe that wishes only the best for you, linking to it through the crystals in your hands. Smile and open your heart to receive that abundance – hold your crystals to your heart as you do so.*
- *Now take that smile down into the creative centre at the base of your belly and allow your hand and your crystals to rest in your lap.*
- *Keeping hold of your stones in one hand, use the other to place the stones.*
- *Lay your Tiger's Eye stone at the centre of the spiral. As*

you lay it, focus your attention on the abundance that surrounds you right now, your base security. Feel how grounded and supported you are by the earth beneath your feet, how rich you already are at your root. If you become aware of any financial worries intruding, let the stone reassure you, feel its strength and security and surrender the worries to the stone and bathe in its abundant energy.

- *Now take the hand holding the crystals up to just below your navel. Pick out the Carnelian and hold it in your other hand for a moment. Feel its bright energy radiating out and allow yourself to absorb that energy so that it activates your abundance attractor factor. Place the stone on the cord spiral and focus your attention on how you attract even more abundance in your life, how you open to receive this beautiful gift of the universe.*

- *Now take your hand and crystals up to your solar plexus. Hold the Citrine and feel the generosity of its energy radiating out from the stone. Feel the bubbles of joy it imparts to your solar plexus. Place the Citrine on the spiral and feel the emotional abundance in your life, the good friends, the family, the warm feelings that support you and your own emotional generosity. Give thanks for those friends and that emotional abundance, and the generosity of spirit that you share.*

- *Now take your crystals up to your heart and hold your Jade in your other hand. As you place the Jade on the spiral let it absorb and transform any fear or self-pity of* which you may have become aware, and assist you to receive with grace and thankfulness. Then ask the stone to help you to find the richness in your heart and open that out to draw abundance to you at every level.

- Finally, take your hand with the Goldstone up above your head. Feel the transmutative energy of the Goldstone radiating down through the core of your being, connecting you to spiritual abundance that floods through every level of your life. As you place the stone at the end of the spiral, let that spiritual abundance flow out into the world and to the future. See its sparkling particles seeding that future with even more abundance, simply waiting for you to reach it and effortlessly harvest it and incorporate it into your life.

- Now bring your attention to the treasure map that is underpinning your spiral. Picture the spiral turning and bringing all those abundant things into your life right now, manifesting more and more of your abundance into your present reality. Feel how this abundance enriches your life. Enjoy!

- Gazing at your spiral, recognise how from being grounded in the creative root of your being you expand and flow outwards and upwards, becoming more and more abundant in your life and sharing that abundance generously with your world.

- Thank the crystals for helping you and, if possible, leave the spiral in place to do its work.

The generating money grid

Crystal potency and intention generate cash. How easily you are able to generate money depends on several things but one of the major causes of not generating money is the belief you have about yourself so the first part of the grid once again involves transmuting those toxic programmes. It also helps to believe that money flows to you through the blessing of the universe: you don't have to work for every penny. The second part involves laying a grid in your home or your place of work. The expansive energy of sacred geometry assists your intention to manifest as you lay out a grid. The mandala shown opposite is based on the Flower of Life, which contains a Merkaba, Metatron's Cube, the Star of David and other metaphysical shapes including the radiating spirals below. (See *The Ultimate Guide to Crystal Grids: Transform Your Life Using the Power of Crystals and Layouts*.)

Choose places for the crystals where they will not be disturbed and remember to cleanse them regularly.

You will need: Aventurine, Turquoise or other appropriate stone (raw chunks or tumblestones can be used). As the grid follows the Chinese Feng Shui grid, you could choose stones that correspond to each area of life (see page 145 and the A–Z Directory).

Timing: If using Turquoise or white stones for this grid, perform it at new moon. If using other stones, lay it out between new and full moon.

Preparation. Reviewing your script: Take time to review the script that runs in your head without you really being conscious of it, the kind of things that you were told in childhood or which your culture imbues you with, the negative expectations you have. Before you go any further ask yourself if you've ever said or been told:

- You have to work incredibly hard to have money
- There'll never be enough
- People like us don't do things like that
- Money is the root of all evil
- The world owes me a living
- "I'll never get out of debt"
- "I don't deserve that"
- You're not good enough
- There's virtue in poverty
- "I'm not clever enough/good enough"
- That's my dream but it won't generate money so I can't do it
- You can't turn your passion into a career
- Be realistic
- "I don't have the right accent and clothes to do that kind of a job"
- "I didn't go to the right kind of school so I'll never have/get a good job"

- "I can only be happy if I have money"

If necessary, use the exercise overleaf to change your mental blueprint before you lay out the generating money grid.

Exercise: changing your mental blueprint

- *Revisit pages 70–71 and pages 78–81, and take another look at some of the fixed points on your mental blueprint, those toxic thoughts imprinted in childhood and by your cultural core beliefs. To release these, hold a prosperity or other appropriate stone in your hand, close your eyes and think about each negative belief. As you do so, deliberately choose the opposite belief. Say out loud the positive belief and lay down the crystal on the mandala opposite to affirm the positive belief that replaces the negative. Repeat for each negative belief so that you build up a new mental blueprint for yourself, one that is abundant and prosperous and which leaves room for all the other things that enrich your life.*
    - *Now open your eyes and look at how many positive beliefs enrich your life. You may like to make a mandala (see full page illustration) with the stones in the success part of your house and leave them in place to remind you of how rich your life is.*
- *The mandala makes a perfect focus for daily meditation. When you have placed your crystals, gaze at it, letting your eyes go out of focus, and quietening your breathing while you observe the stones. Do not try to make*

anything happen, simply allow. Notice how different
you feel after a week.

The generating money grid

You will need:
8 abundance stones
Keystone
Anchor stone

The grid placement: You could choose the wealth corner
(see page 145) for this or place it on the template.
Orientate the grid so that the top point (point A) corre-
sponds to the wealth corner of your house or room – the
far left-hand corner at the back – and place it where it
will not be disturbed. If you have bought a lottery ticket,
place it in the centre of the grid. Place your crystals
intuitively on the points that draw you to them.

- *Focus your intention and lay your first stone on the grid*
  saying out loud, "I am generating money, I set this gener-
  ation in motion now."
- *Lay your second stone saying: "Money grows ever*
  larger."
- *Lay your third stone and say: "Money grows without*
  boundaries."
- *Lay your fourth stone and say: "Money arrives from*
  unexpected sources."
- *Lay your fifth stone and say: "Money flows freely."*
- *Lay your sixth stone and say: "Money increases moment*

by moment."

- *Lay your seventh stone and say: "Money grows and grows."*
- *Lay your eighth stone and say: "Money flows freely to me from all directions in all ways."*
- *Look at the centre of the grid and picture a huge pile of money growing and growing until it spills abundantly all over the grid. Feel that money growing and your sense of joyful abundance increasing.*
- *Take a moment to say thank you for the abundance that flows to you.*
- *Place a keystone in the centre and an anchoring stone outside the grid.*
- *Withdraw your attention and your emotion.*
- *Leave the grid to do its work.*

The Flower of Life containing a Merkaba, Metatron's Cube, the Star of David and other metaphysical shapes. Begin your grid at the centre with a keystone or at point A (top of the grid).

The Prosperity Ritual

Deep introspection into what you truly believe is an essential part of this prosperity ritual: an examination that takes at least three days – for which the dark period between the death of the old moon and the rise of the new is a perfect space as it assists you to go inwards to explore your deepest beliefs. Once you have focused your mind and feelings on to what prosperity really means for you, you are ready to carry out this ritual.

You will need:
White or silver notebook and pen
Mineral salts or Halite crystal
White flowers, candles and holders, cloth, crystals such as Quartz, Clear Elestial Quartz, Moonstone, Selenite, White Calcite, White Jade

Timing: Use the three dark days of the old moon to examine your beliefs about prosperity. Perform the ritual at new moon rise to sow the seeds of your prosperity or at full moon to bring a project to fruition.

Preparation: Read through your answers to the questions posed in Sections 2 and 3. From these responses and any additional insights, consider exactly what prosperity means to you. Initially, write your thoughts as a 'stream of consciousness' in which everything you personally believe and think about prosperity pours on to the page. Don't censor and don't judge what you write, simply allow it to be. When you're sure you've emptied all your thoughts and beliefs about prosperity into the notebook, read through what you've written from a standpoint of compassionate witnessing. That is, don't judge yourself for having these thoughts and beliefs. Recognise that they are simply that – thoughts and beliefs. You are more than these programmes your mind is running. Be gentle with yourself. Distil the major points and write them in your notebook in the form of statements such as:

"I believe that prosperity is ...."
"To me, prosperity means ...."
"To be prosperous I have to: ...."
"I do not feel prosperous because ...."
"I am already prosperous because ...."
"I feel that other people are prosperous because ...."

And any more headings that are appropriate.

Now hold a prosperity crystal and breathe into your heart, focus all your attention there and allow your heart to expand. Feel yourself connecting to your deep inner self that is beyond your ego or your personality. From a place of the love within your heart and your true self for the you that is having all these struggles and beliefs, go through the list and ask yourself how much you truly believe in these things. You can also ask yourself from where these thoughts and beliefs about prosperity stem. You'll no doubt find that many of them have been inculcated into your mind by your parents and the people around you when you were a child or a young adult. If you no longer accept them as true, ask yourself what is true for you now in this present moment and write those answers into your notebook. Sleep on your answers overnight and then read them through again, and ask yourself once more: "Is this really true for me now?" If it is, write it on a new page. If it's not, write in what is true for you at this moment in time. Distil the essence of these statements into a sentence that begins:

"For me true prosperity is ...."

Place: If the weather is suitable this ritual is particularly potent carried out somewhere in nature where your crystals are under the direct light of the full or the rising new moon. If not, then choose a windowsill that faces the rising moon if possible on which to place your crystals.

The Prosperity Ritual:

- *Prepare yourself carefully. If the weather is warm and there is a suitable place, you could bathe yourself and your crystals in the sea, a lake or a river. If not, have a bath with a handful of mineral salts or hang a small bag of salt or Halite under the showerhead to wash over you as you shower.*

- *Dedicate your crystals and charge them with the*

intention that you attract to yourself and discover within you true prosperity.

- Place your candles around you, and as you light each one say aloud: "I ignite the flame of true prosperity within myself and invite it to manifest in the world."
- Take the piece of paper on which you have written what true prosperity means to you and read it out loud. Then place it in the centre.
- Take your white flowers and place them around the paper saying out loud, "I invite the powers of nature to unite with me in true prosperity."
- Finally, surround your piece of paper with white crystals and, if you have a large crystal, place this in the centre. As you blow out the candles, state out loud that you invite prosperity into your life right now.
- Leave the crystals in place for two weeks. If the flowers wither, compost them saying, "Let these flowers make fertile compost for my prosperity."
- Each time you notice how much more prosperous you feel in any way, make a note of it in your notebook thanking the crystals for their work in drawing this to you.
- After two weeks, thank the crystals for their work and dismantle the circle. Take the crystals out and 'plant' them somewhere in nature. Place the paper in your notebook.
- Allow your prosperity to grow without investing emotional energy into the outcome.

The Inner-wealth Ritual

True wealth has nothing to do with how much money we have in the bank. It is the qualities within us and those we share with the world around us, our hidden resources that make us truly wealthy. But! Our inner riches are often so well hidden that we only perceive them in other people – or we do not give value to what we have until we think deeply about it and recognise that good friends, for instance, are part of our wealth. This ritual helps you to find these inner riches for yourself.

You will need:
Notebook and pen
Jade, Topaz or other introspective prosperity crystal
Candle and holder

Timing: Dark of the moon: the three days just before new moon.

Preparation: Set aside time when you can be peacefully introspective with no interruptions. You can either do the preparatory work for this ritual in two parts on separate days, allowing time for new insights to arise, or you could do it over the day before new moon doing the first part in the morning, the second in the afternoon and the third in the evening. This allows time for new insights to arise, but you can also add insights that arise after the ritual if you leave space in your notebook and claim these qualities as your own.

What do I see in you?

- *Turn back to the list you made of ten people you admire (see pages 82–83) and write this in your notebook spacing the names out well.*
- *What were the particular qualities that made these people special to you? Note them against each name.*
- *What do these people specifically contribute to your life? Make a note.*

We frequently admire in other people qualities that we seek, but do not yet recognise, in ourselves. So:

- *Is there a specific quality or qualities that come up time and again? If so, note it below the list under a heading 'Qualities I need to own in myself'.*

We often contribute more than we realise to the lives of other people. So:

- *If the people on your list are personally known to you, ask them to list what you contribute to their lives.*
- *Do you recognise these qualities in yourself?*

And finally:

- *Write down your twenty best qualities.*

- *Ask a friend to write down your twenty best qualities.*
- *How do they compare?*
- *Ask yourself: "Do I believe them?"*

Questions to ponder

- Have I tapped into my inner worth?
- Do I truly value me?
- Do I have good friends?
- Is there a way to increase my friendship quotient?
- How mutual are my friendships?
- Does everything go one way in my friendships?
- Is this flow to me or away from me?
- Do I need to shed some of my old needy friends and find new ones?
- Do I make time in my life for enriching activities?
- If not, can I program time in?
- Do I meditate or have another spiritual practice?
- How do I serve others?
- Could I volunteer in any capacity?
- What activities could I engage in that would enrich my life?
- Do I engage in creative activities?
- Did I engage in creative activities as a child or young adult?
- If there are things I'd like to do but don't, what's stopping me?

The Inner-wealth Ritual:

- *If you find background music relaxing, play something slow and introspective that helps you to move deeper into yourself. Dim the lights.*
- *Settle yourself comfortably where you will not be disturbed and light your candle. Place it in front of you.*
- *Read through your notebook and, on a separate piece of paper, make a list of all the qualities that you admire or that you see within yourself and others.*
- *Pick up your piece of Jade, breathe gently and relax. Spend a few moments looking at your piece of Jade. Feel its quiet confidence, its strength and its serenity. Let these qualities travel through your hands, up your arms and into your heart.*
- *When you are ready, pick up your list of qualities in your other hand and look at the first one. Can you own it within yourself? If yes, touch the Jade to your heart, say out loud, "I own and honour my [   ]." Tick off the quality on your list, and move on to the next one.*
- *If no, then quietly affirm to yourself: "I am/have [   ], I own my [   ], my [   ] is part of my inner wealth, I honour my [   ], I am grateful for my [   ] and I am ready to show my [   ] to the world." When you believe it, touch your Jade to your heart, tick off the quality on your list and move on.*
- *So, for example: I have integrity, I own my integrity, my integrity is part of my inner wealth, I honour my integrity, I am grateful for my integrity, and I am ready*

to show my integrity to the world.

- Repeat this affirmation for every quality on your list. If you find it difficult to own qualities, simply sit quietly repeating to yourself, "I am [ ]," until you believe it.

- So, for example, "I am integrity, I am integrity, I am integrity..."

- Then repeat the whole affirmation out loud, touch the Jade to your heart and put a big tick by the quality on your list.

- When you have completed the list, spend a few moments contemplating this reservoir of inner wealth. All these enriching qualities within you. This heartfelt store of riches.

- When you are ready to end the ritual, blow out the candle saying: "I send my riches out to the world in blessing and in gratitude."

- Place the list where you see it often and place the Jade under your pillow.

- Enjoy your inner wealth and let it shine out to the world.

Asking for blessings on a new venture

Blessings were sought in ancient times when people petitioned the gods for good fortune for a new venture. Their chosen tool was a crystal – stones still exist with such petitions engraved on them. Nowadays it is more usual to ask for an angel blessing than a god but you can request a blessing from whichever divine being resonates with you, or from the universe itself.

Crystal shapes are particularly useful for inaugurating new ventures. An egg shape is like a seed, it hatches into something bigger when the time is right. A sphere represents fullness, it has no limitations, all possibilities are open and can be realised. A point draws the energy in or sends it out to the universe depending on which way it is pointing.

You will need: Iron Pyrite, Moonstone, Turquoise, White Calcite or other stone of new beginnings. An egg or sphere shape is ideal.

Timing: New ventures are best started on a new moon or in the period leading up to a full moon. Avoid starting a new venture on a waning moon or during the dark of the moon or the period leading up to the winter solstice (although this is an ideal time for preparatory contemplation of the venture). Astrologically speaking, new ventures are particularly auspicious when started at the commencement of a new Jupiter cycle which takes place every twelve years, so at age 12, 24, 36, 48, 60, 72 and 84. Jupiter is the 'major beneficent' correlating with abundance and expansion. (Just as I was writing this piece, a friend emailed to say that the *Last Night of the Proms* was playing Holst's *Jupiter*. A highly auspicious, serendipitous synchronicity.)

Preparation: Before you ask for the blessing, take time for introspection. Ensure that your venture accords with your ideals and your deepest integrity. Set out your intentions for the venture clearly. Your venture does not have to be something that earns money but if it does and you need to earn a specific amount, specify this and add "or something greater". If you are intending to help people, make that a goal. Cleanse your crystal and magnetise it for success before commencing the blessing.

The blessing: Holding your crystal in your hands, call down the blessing of the universe on your venture and into the crystal. So for example you could use:

> *I ask the great Jupiter to pour blessings on my new venture for the highest good of all concerned, bringing it success and abundance now and always, and I ask that this crystal attunes to your blessing and radiates it out for the benefit of all. [If you need anything specific add it here.] Thank*

you, Jupiter, for your assistance in this venture.

Place your crystal in an appropriate place such as the success portion of your home or place of work.

Treasure maps

Treasure maps are fun to make and should be made with focused intention. Treasure maps help you to focus on exactly what you would like to manifest and to be specific in your choices. Collect pictures or phrases together that illustrate exactly what you want. Look through old magazines or brochures, and keep an eye out for anything appropriate. If you're looking for your ideal house, for instance, collect pictures of houses that appeal to you, floor plans that work for you and interior design ideas you'd like to incorporate. Use PVA glue to stick appropriate crystals on the map.

You will need:
Large piece of card or a large clip frame
Pictures or photographs
Small pieces of crystal
Glue stick and/or PVA glue

Timing: You can make a treasure map at any time.

Treasure Map:

- *Lay out your pictures to the same size as your card or clip frame first so that you make a pleasing arrangement. If appropriate, place a photo of yourself in the centre; choose a happy smiling one.*
- *Carefully glue the pictures and phrases on to your card.*

As you place them say to yourself: "I am creating exactly what I want, I call this into being now."

Decorate the clip frame by gluing small pieces of crystal around the edge or place the card into a frame on to which you have glued crystals. Display it where you see it often but remember not to make an emotional investment into the outcome. You succeed far more quickly if you remain detached.

Managing your money

Managing your money means more than simply having a budget and sticking to it. There are always unexpected demands on your purse but if you are in an ever-flowing energy stream, the money and the resources you need are irresistibly attracted towards you and there is always enough to go round. If you suffer from scarcity mentality, now is the time to change your thinking.

Sensible spending

Wearing Green Quartz, also known as Prasiolite, helps you to stop haemorrhaging money and to make sensible budgetary choices. It also assists you to be charitable, both to yourself and others. Jet and Peridot are ancient aids to stabilising your finances.

To plan a budget

Green Spinel assists in budgeting and sorting out a financial mess, as does Cinnabar (*toxic: use tumbled and wash hands after use*) or Peridot. Hold the crystal for a few moments and allow creative solutions to rise up into your mind. Wear a bracelet of magnetised prosperity stones to remind you of your budget when in areas of temptation such as shops and when browsing the Internet. (*See Managing your money page 254.*)

To become more creative with your money

Finding new ways to grow your money without risks is

assisted by Goldstone or Malachite. Hold the crystal in your hands and ask that the way be opened to creative use of your money. Watch for opportunities that come your way. Peridot is a crystal of financial and spiritual abundance. It assists you to leave behind your old habits such as spending too much or being miserly, and shows how to be creative with what you have. This stone puts out to the universe that you are ready to accept abundance right now.

Chakra support system: Poverty consciousness is a base, sacral and dantien chakra issue. To reverse a sense of lack or a blocked energy flow, place brown crystals over the earth chakra beneath your feet, red crystals over your base chakra, orange over your sacral and green or pink over your heart. To stimulate the earth chakra and ground yourself in the material world, place brown crystals and earthy grounding stones such as Hematite on your feet. To stimulate power in your dantien, place Red Jasper, Fire Agate or other energizing crystal just below your navel.

Suggested exercises: Prosperity ritual page 166, Inner-wealth ritual page 168, Abundance Layout page 156, Generating money grid page 159, Wealth Corner page 145.

Attracting the money you need

As we have seen, prosperity is not purely a matter of having money but there are times when you may need a chunk of cash in a hurry. The stones in this section also attract other resources you may need.

Attracting money

Put a Citrine, Jet or Yellow Sapphire in your purse or cashbox and Carnelian in the entrance to your home to attract money. Green Grossular Garnet manifests the money you need for necessities or fun. Place Garnets in a Star of David pattern, one triangle over another around a note of the amount of money and what you specifically require it for. If possible, place it under a new moon. Peridot attracts money you need, creating a healthy flow if you keep one in your purse or on bills awaiting payment.

If money is slow to arrive

Visualise a large spiral of Green Spinels spinning rapidly over your bed to bring you a delayed payment, legacy or other money that is slow in coming. Picture another spiral over the letterbox to draw in wins on a lottery, premium bond or other randomly generated opportunity. *(See also the Repayment of a debt layout on page 182.)*

To use money wisely

Green Tourmaline helps to appreciate what you have and

to allocate your money in the wisest way so that you always have enough. It assists in being creative in how you manage your money, opening your eyes to new possibilities whether for recycling what you have, bartering or other energy exchange, or spotting a new opportunity such as volunteering that keeps the energy flowing. Prehnite supports your ability to take sensible risks and encourages your own inner knowing to prompt you when a not-to-be-missed-opportunity comes along.

Chakra support system: Creation and attraction is a sacral chakra issue and orange stones placed on this area assist you to draw in all the money and other resources that you need.

Suggested exercises: Prosperity ritual page 166, Inner-wealth ritual page 168, Abundance Layout page 156, Generating money grid page 159, Wealth Corner page 145.

Repayment of a debt

If repayment of a loan or other debt, or payment of an invoice, is slow in coming or the debtor is reluctant to pay, you can lay out a grid to bring the money back to you. If you have an unpaid invoice or other paperwork, you could lay the grid on it. Enclosing the grid in a ring of Amber and Black Tourmaline, Shungite or other protective stone prevents any fallout or 'blowback' radiating, or lashing out, from the debtor to adversely affect yourself or people around you. 'Blowback' is the unintended adverse results of an action or situation. It can be experienced as 'negative reactions or results that were not intended, such as criticism, protest, or anger'. It may well bring up old karma and ancestral patterns, karmic and ancestral soul contracts, thought forms and toxic emotions to be dealt with if there was a personal or soul-contract element to the debt (see pages 113 and 119). However, the consequences may also be positive – debts that you had forgotten about finally being repaid in one way or another. Adding Petaltone Essence's Plant Ally to the centre stone can be effective in such cases. As would placing a piece of Anandalite or other light-bringing or space-holding stone under the central Sapphire.

You will need:
Pentangle base layout (see page 39)
1 Sapphire keystone (raw or faceted) plus light-bringer if required

Sufficient Blue Kyanite blades to lay out the pentangle
5 pieces of Amber
5 Flint stones
Sufficient Black Tourmaline or Shungite to form a ring around grid
A Kyanite wand

Method:

- *Cleanse the crystals and hold them in your hand.*
- *Say out loud: "I ask these crystals to draw back to me the money that is owed as quickly and smoothly as possible." (You can put a time limit if appropriate.)*
- *Lay the Sapphire in the centre of the pentangle. (Place on top of Anandalite or Selenite if you need to bring light into the situation.)*
- *Lay Kyanite blades along the lines of the pentangle.*
- *Join up the pentangle with a Kyanite wand (you can use another Kyanite blade).*
- *Feel the money begin to make its way back to you.*
- *Lay a piece of Amber on every point.*
- *Join up the Amber by making a circle with Black Tourmaline or Shungite around the grid.*
- *Lay a piece of Flint outside the layout level with each point to anchor the grid.*
- *Leave the grid undisturbed and remove your attention to allow the crystals to do their work.*

Inner peace

Peace is a wealth that no one can take away from you and only you can find in the stillness of your inner being. With inner peace safely anchored in your heart, nothing knocks you off balance or makes you doubt yourself. Richness indeed. Spending fifteen minutes with your crystals night and morning helps you to still your mind and reach this peace deep within yourself. Wearing one constantly reminds you of your unshakeable core of inner peace.

Crystal meditation for inner peace

At the most simple level, keeping your crystal with you at all times and gently stroking it or turning it in your hand clears your mind and focuses your attention in the present moment. Take three slow, deep, mindful breaths as you do so. But you can also 'crystal gaze' to find inner peace. The intention is not to 'zone out' but rather to become more present. 'Palm stones', flat, rounded shapes, are specially made to facilitate this way of using your crystal and are often known as 'worry stones', although anti-worry would be a better description. They are excellent if you feel anxious or worried but they also act as reminders to stay in the present moment. A large tumblestone or ball works equally well.

- Hold the crystal loosely in your hands just below eye level in front of you.

- Allow your eyes to go into soft focus and gently scan the crystal until your eyes naturally come to rest.
- Continue gazing into the crystal until your mind clears, your breathing slows and you relax, fully present in the moment.

This method works well with crystals such as Anandalite, Amethyst, Eye of the Storm, Labradorite, Porcelain Jasper, Prairie Tanzanite, Quartz, Selenite, or, if strong emotions prevent inner peace and need releasing, Malachite.

To find inner serenity

Jade is a traditional serenity stone highly regarded for its connection to wisdom garnered in tranquillity. Eye of the Storm (Judy's Jasper) is a very recent discovery that places you in a clear, calm space and allows you to take an overview on your prosperity as does the newly-discovered Prairie Tanzanite. Contemplate the stone several times a day to connect to inner peace. Wearing Jade or Eye of the Storm maintains inner peace during difficult times. Rose Quartz is a stone of infinite compassion and deep peace that attunes you to unconditional, universal love and helps you to love yourself. Calcite calms your whole being so that you sink into a deeply peaceful state and attune yourself to unconditional love and stillness. Following the spiral of an Ammolite inwards with your eyes takes you into a place of profound peace and tranquillity. Here you release anything that troubles you and transmute your fears into infinite peace. Uvarovite Garnet transforms loneliness into an appreciation for solitude and the strength you gain in being alone. Amethyst has long been valued for helping you to still your mind and reach spiritual connection through meditation. Wear an Amethyst to remind you of your deep well of inner peace. Chrysoprase helps you to feel part of the greater whole and induces a deep meditation state. If you find it difficult to relax and enter a meditative state, it helps you to let go and feel the divine flow.

Chakra support system: Inner peace rests in your heart and heart seed chakras. Place pink stones over your heart and green stones over the heart seed to draw in and anchor deep peace at the centre of your being.

Suggested exercises: Inner-wealth ritual page 168, Crystal meditation page 184.

Finding a fulfilling job

Different crystals accord with your short-term aims and others with a longer view. All crystals help you to maintain a good balance between your working life and your home or leisure time. You can place stones in the career and success areas of your home (the central front and back portions of your home, *see page 145*).

To attract a new job

Adamite is useful if you know exactly what job you seek. Place one over the advertisement for a job before you attend an interview. If you cannot find Adamite, use a piece of Iron Pyrite or Magnetite. If you have long-term career plans, magnetise a piece of Tree or other Agate to keep you on track as you work towards your goal. This earthy stone, or Moss Agate, is appropriate for working outdoors especially in forestry, agriculture or horticulture as it increases fertility of anything that grows. As it also enhances your communication with living beings, it is helpful for veterinary or zoological-associated careers also. (*And see page 243.*)

To enhance your employment prospects

Invest in some Black Sapphire or Jet jewellery or put a piece of the darkest blue raw Sapphire you can find by your front door to enhance your employment prospects and to retain the job once you secure it. Cinnabar *(caution toxic)* makes your demeanour elegant and pleasing to the beholder so it is useful when you want to enhance your appearance for jobs in which appearance matters (place it opposite to your front door, *see page 145 and wash your hands after handling it*).

To help you study

If you need to pass an examination before you achieve your goal, Amazez, Calcite or Fluorite focuses your mind, as does Chalcedony.

Chakra support system: Stimulate and energize your base chakra with red stones and your throat with blue stones so that you fully communicate your skills and insights to prospective employers.

Finding the perfect job ritual

Perfect jobs are out there for everyone. This ritual draws on the previous work you have done and requires you to focus even deeper into what it is you really want. It is equally as suitable for finding your dream career as it is for a fill-in job while at college. Both are as fulfilling as possible and bring you what you need.

You will need:
Small gold notebook and pen
Golden cloth
6 Golden Tiger's Eye tumblestones
Gold candle in a suitable holder and matches

Note: You can use Red Tiger's Eye if you feel more attracted to this colour, in which case choose a dark red or pink notebook, cloth and candle for the ritual.

Timing: This ritual is particularly effective at new moon but it works whenever you feel ready to do it. You could prepare in the days leading up the new moon, doing a question before you go to bed, or you could do the whole thing in a day. Sleep on the answers for at least one night to allow fresh insights to arise before you complete the ritual.

Preparation: Take your phone off the hook and put a do not disturb notice on your door. Ensure that you have allocated sufficient time whether you are completing the preparation and ritual in one session or in smaller sections.

If you find music soothing, play suitable background music or prepare in silence.

Sit quietly and focus your thoughts inward. Let the distractions of the outer world slip away.

Remind yourself that your intent is to find a new and fulfilling job, and that the ritual is to bring that job into manifestation.

Breathe gently focusing on your breath. As you breathe out, allow any tension you may be feeling to drop away. As you breathe in, feel yourself filling up with a sense of peace and relaxation.

When you feel ready, pick up your pen and notebook,

and ask yourself what you most want out of a job. Be specific and precise but don't censor what comes into your mind. Be open to all possibilities and paradoxes, you can always train or retrain. If you have a particular salary in mind, say so but don't limit it, "above $/£/currency per year" opens the possibility of a higher salary than you envisage.

- If you want to work in a specific location, pinpoint it – or open it up to wherever is appropriate for you.
- If you need a particular level of responsibility, specify it. If job satisfaction matters most to you, say so, and so on.
- But remember, if what you are looking for is simply a fill-in job, something to generate money for the time being, or a step in the right direction but not your ultimate goal, this is acceptable too. Simply be honest with yourself about it and include the time frame "for the time being" or, if possible, give yourself a time frame that says, "… and by [specify date] I move on from this job to something even better."
- Leaving the first page blank, write each point in your notebook. Give it plenty of space. Let it breathe.
- Then list all the skills and experience you bring to this new job.
- Now think about your goals and write those in the

notebook. Be specific about your timing, objectives, anticipated outcome. Remember to add "this or something better".

- Contemplate alternatives and think laterally. Is there a different area in which you could use your skills? Could you retrain? Is there something you've always wanted to do but never had the opportunity? List it all!

- Now check out any inherent contradictions you may have within what you have written. Ask yourself if the desired outcome is in accord with your highest ideals and your deepest integrity. If there is a contradiction, how do you feel about it? Does expediency trump ideology? Can you encompass the contradictions for the time being? Or are there areas where you just cannot go? If there are, list them. Be absolutely clear what is acceptable to you and what is not.

- When you have finished writing, place the notebook under your pillow and tell yourself that during the night any further insights that you need rise up into your consciousness and that you remember them so that you note them when you wake. Pay particular attention to any dreams that you may have and make a note of these *whether or not they seem relevant at the time*.

The Perfect Job ritual:

- *Have a bath or shower and put on clean clothes.*
- *Dim the lights and, if you wish, play suitable background music or work the ritual in silence.*
- *Now take your notebook and read through it.*
- *Distil the essence of what you want from this new job into one sentence and write it in the front of your notebook, starting, "My new job is......" (You may also like to make a note on a piece of paper so that you read it aloud as part of the ritual.)*
- *Spread the cloth on to a table and place the candle on the notebook in the centre. Around the candle slowly and deliberately place the six Tiger's Eyes in a Star of David pattern (two overlapping triangles one point up to release your intention out to the universe, the second point down to draw it into manifestation, see page 38.) As you place the stones say, "I place these stones to bring my new job into manifestation."*
- *Then light the candle and look deep into the flame.*
- *Affirm to yourself that the job is already there ready for you, waiting to come into manifestation right now.*
- *Call your new job into being. Putting as much feeling and intention as possible into it, read out the sentence that sums up the essence of your new job, starting, "My new job is..." and ending, "and I call it into being now."*
- *Put your hand on your heart and picture being in this job, how you feel, the satisfaction and excitement it*

gives you. See yourself doing the job as the future stretches out before you and pull that future into the ever present now. Put as much emotion as possible into the seeing.

- When you are ready, blow the candle out sending your intention for this job into the universe with the smoke. Thank the universe for granting your request. Be confident that it returns to you in tangible form. Let it go.

- Leave the notebook in the centre of the stones for several days. Each morning light the candle and call your new job into being, feeling delighted anticipation as you do so. Thank the universe for listening. Then blow out the candle, let go, and trust that it manifests in the best way possible for you.

- Each time you blow the candle out, remove your focus and your emotion from the Star of David but be ready to spot any opportunity that comes your way.

Increasing your success

Increasing your success depends on how you define success. Be specific as to whether you want success in the material world, in growing as a person, opening your spiritual gifts, finding love, meeting your goals and so on when magnetising your success stones.

Finding material success

Cinnabar *(caution toxic)* draws success to endeavours and assists in turning fortune around, finding success in unexpected places. Tree Agate slowly draws material success to you. Carnelian stimulates success in business as does Citrine and Jet. To maintain humility when you find success, wear Spinels. If man-made they remind you that not everything can be judged as to quality and genuineness by outside appearances. Square-cut Garnets should be worn to ensure success in business. To activate your will to succeed, hold beautiful pink Morganite.

Finding creative success

Aventurine is useful if you are seeking success in creative endeavours, as is Dendritic Agate. This stone of plenitude brings abundance to all areas of life. It helps you to be prolific and inventive, and enjoy every moment of your creative life.

Succeeding in your goals

If you have specific goals wear vibrant Topaz, Ruby,

Tiger's Eye or Citrine to bring them to fruition. Hemimorphite helps set realistic goals without emotional attachment while Red Chalcedony encourages persistence in achieving goals.

Successful love

Wear Emerald to maintain your love and Rose Quartz to enhance your success in love. It helps you to fulfil other ambitions too.

Spiritual success

Making a breakthrough in your spiritual understanding is facilitated by Morganite. Once you see past the material world many things drop into place. To open spiritual awareness, place Ammolite or Moonstone over your third eye. To access another dimension of consciousness, place Ammolite, Lapis Lazuli or Turquoise on your crown chakra.

Chakra support system: Stimulate your solar plexus chakra with yellow stones and your sacral chakra with orange ones for material success. For success in love, place appropriate green or pink stones over your heart and for spiritual success white, lilac or pale blue stones over your heart, soma and crown chakras.

Suggested exercises: Gratitude and blessings page 140, Inner-wealth ritual page 168, Asking for blessings on a new venture page 173, Treasure maps page 176.

Achieving your dreams

Dreams are a fragile and wondrous thing. We need to distinguish between what is an achievable dream and what is an illusion. Crystals assist in making this distinction. Acting as symbols of what might come into being, crystal eggs nurture and give birth to your dreams. Points draw dreams towards you.

Bringing dreams into being

Calcite gives courage to act and courage to be whatever you dream of becoming. It acts as a stepping stone between a dream and its fruition, releasing limiting beliefs holding you back. Smoky Quartz manifests dreams and makes them a reality. Jade nurtures your dreams and brings them to fruition. If you need assistance in devising a strategy to make a dream a reality, use Red Chalcedony. Wear Ruby to remain emotionally detached from the outcome.

Incubating a dream

If you are not quite sure what you dream of for yourself, magnetise an Aventurine or Moonstone crystal and place it under your pillow. Keep a pen and paper beside the bed to write down the dream as soon as you wake. Remember that many dreams are symbols of other things.

Separating an achievable dream from an illusion

Moonstone is an excellent dreaming tool but may induce illusions in sensitive people rather than an achievable reality. Black or Pink Moonstone is useful in such cases. Purple Tourmaline or Carnelian strips away illusions and reveals the stark reality behind your dreams. But if the dream is realistic, Carnelian helps it to manifest.

Chakra support system: To manifest your dreams place your crystals over your heart and on the soma chakra at the midpoint of your hairline above and between your eyebrows (above the third eye) and then at your feet to ground them into the physical manifestation.

Suggested exercises: Generating money grid page 159, Finding the perfect job ritual page 188, Treasure maps page 176.

Buying that car

Honesty with yourself is needed when buying your car. What you are seeking – and why? Do you simply want a reliable means of transport from one place to another? Or do you want a flashy ego-boosting status symbol that tells the world you've arrived? There's nothing wrong with this if it's joyfully celebrating your success, but you need to be honest with yourself and check that it's not a substitute for true self-esteem. Have you always dreamed of a particular car? Once you clarify the under-lying reason for buying, different crystals placed on a treasure map support your choice.

Buying your dream car

Acting as a stepping stone between a dream and its fruition, Calcite assists a search for what you have longed for. Choose an appropriate colour: Red Calcite if it's a flashy status symbol, Black Calcite for a more restrained one. For a romantic dream, choose Mangano Calcite, and for a practical workhorse, Brown Calcite. Smoky Quartz too manifests your dreams and Red Chalcedony devises strategies for successful acquisition.

Buying a status symbol

As Ruby is a stone of wealth and prestige, it assists finding a car you are passionate about, one that makes you feel really wealthy. Chrysoprase helps you to ascertain whether a status symbol car is merely an ego-booster or would bring the recognition you seek.

Buying an environmentally friendly car

Indicolite (Blue) Tourmaline helps buy a car that is in harmony with the environment. Jade is useful if the idea of an environmentally friendly car is new to you; it kickstarts considering the environment more as do Aventurine and Moss Agate. Dendritic Agate assists in considerate harvesting of resources. To keep your car working reliably, place Smoky Quartz in it. Quartz taped to the fuel line amplifies the mileage.

Chakra support system: For finding an appropriate means of transport from A to B, place brown stones over your earth chakra. For your dream car, place an appropriate stone over your soma chakra first. For a flashy status symbol, place appropriate stones on the base, sacral and earth chakras.

Suggested exercises: Treasure maps page 176, Gratitude and blessings page 140, Changing the world with intent page 14, Generating money grid page 159.

Rediscovering your skills

Rediscovering lost skills and abilities enriches you beyond measure and it's never too late to expand upon an interest or ability you have lost touch with. To find one thing that, even for one brief shining moment, you're better at than anyone else makes you feel special: it enriches you within that moment. But there is enormous pleasure to be found in the process of creating whatever form it takes. Go back over your life and remember what you enjoyed and what you were good at no matter how long ago – they may not necessarily be the same and it is by no means essential that they are. You are enriched by doing something simply for the pleasure of doing, not for the finished result.

Creativity

Andradite Garnet or Triplite stimulates creativity and attracts what you most need for your development on all levels. If your creativity has been blocked or simply lost in the mists of time, Tiger's Eye rapidly releases it and helps find a suitable outlet for your creative talents. Wear one to boost your abilities and regain the joy of creation. If it's mental creativity you are seeking, Lapis Lazuli instils clarity and inspiration.

Problem solving and technology

Topaz sharpens your mind and assists in problem solving but is also an excellent stone for anyone engaged in the arts. Aventurine assists you to get to grips with anything technological, enhancing your skills.

Storytelling and active listening

If you've an interest in storytelling, Pink Chalcedony enhances your skills. This stone instils a sense of childlike wonder and encourages being open to new things. Chinese Writing Stone or Calligraphy Stone offer enormous encouragement to write. People benefit immensely from being listened to in an empathetic way and Lapis Lazuli has long been valued for the quality of active listening.

Chakra support system: To discover what you are capable of, place pink crystals over the heart seed chakra at the base of your breastbone, and to regain your power, appropriate crystals over your sacral chakra.

Suggested exercises: Inner-wealth ritual page 168.

Improving your work-leisure balance

Encompassing work as a part of your overall life keeps a balance. Crystals assist in feeling there is sufficient time for everything – it is part of living abundantly. Imbalance can arise out of an inability to say no or set boundaries. Bicoloured crystals facilitate a better balance between different areas of your life when combined with a visualisation technique before you sleep.

Setting boundaries

Agate helps to do only what is necessary and to say no when appropriate. If you need help in setting boundaries and learning how to say no, wear Aventurine constantly and tape one over your spleen. Calcite is useful when you've always been a yes person and need to say no gently but firmly. Lavender Jade helps to set clear boundaries between yourself and others.

Taking time out

If you need time away from work, or from the demands of family, Almandine Garnet supports taking time out for yourself, and Andradite Garnet gives courage to do what whatever is best for you.

Bringing about a balance

- *At night, put Merlinite or Amazez under your pillow.*
- *Close your eyes and picture an old-fashioned pair of scales with pans on each side hanging from a pivot. On one side picture something that represents your working life. On the other something that represents home or leisure time. They will come to a stop with one pan higher than the other.*
- *Add a Merlinite crystal to the higher so that the pans become balanced.*
- *Ask that, in the morning, you intuitively know how to find this balance in your life.*
- *When you wake, note your dreams or other signals as to how you can rearrange your life.*
- *Wear Merlinite to remind you to seek balance or Turquoise or the lovely Sunset Sodalite to find creative solutions to balancing your life.*

Chakra support system: Place a brown crystal on the earth chakra beneath your feet, an orange crystal on your sacral chakra, a pink stone on your heart and a blue stone on your soma chakra.

Suggested exercises: *Gratitude and blessings page 140, Changing the world with intent page 14, Inner-wealth ritual page 168.*

Enriching your relationships

Relationships of all kinds contribute enormously to your sense of inner wealth. As you align yourself more strongly to your inner resources, so your outer vibrations change and attract into your life people who support your worldview and your prosperity.

Position: Place or wear the following stones over your heart.

To attract a twinflame

A soulmate or twinflame crystal has two points springing side by side from the same base. A twinflame is like a soulmate but without the karma. Soulmates can scour our soul. Twinflames enrich heart and soul. Wear Blue Aragonite or Turquoise to attract a twinflame who supports your soul's plan and with whom you share deep love and soul-to-soul communication.

To enhance an existing relationship

Rose Quartz is unconditional love. Its presence creates loving harmony. To rekindle love that is feeling stale, wear Morganite as it increases the sense of value in a relationship. If forgiveness would help, Mangano Calcite is perfect. Place one under your pillow to maintain unconditional love and release anything that may be keeping a relationship mired in an unsatisfactory past. If it's more passion you seek, use Ruby, Garnet, Red Jasper or Green Aventurine.

To attract new friends

Chrysoprase encourages fidelity and integrity, teaching that cooperation is more enriching than competition. It attracts like-minded friends who enjoy sharing mutual interests. Jade is the ultimate friendship stone.

To attract a mentor

A mentor formation is a large crystal taking a small one under its wing and is excellent to magnetise to attract exactly the right spiritual or material teacher. Merlinite attracts a mentor who teaches how to draw on your own inner wisdom.

Chakra support system: To enrich a heart connection, place pink or green crystals over your heart. To enrich a mutually supportive and passionate connection, place red crystals over your base chakra and orange crystals below your navel. To increase an emotional connection, place pink or yellow crystals over your solar plexus.

Suggested exercises: Gratitude and blessings page 140, Abundance layout page 156.

Bringing more joy into your life

Crystals are like little packets of joy and they are only too happy to share their abundant happiness with you. Simply having one near you raises your happiness quotient as they constantly radiate good vibes out into the environment. For best results wear crystals set in gold. Palmstones or 'worry beads' are helpful.

Joy bringers

Citrine, Topaz and Sapphire help you to feel that life is fundamentally joyful. The golden hue of Citrine and Topaz symbolises the sun and everyone feels more joyful in the sunshine, so wear one of these crystals to lift your spirits. Mellow Orange or Yellow Jade have been used to bring more joy into life for thousands of years and were much prized for their ability to promote happiness. All these crystals increase the flow of endorphins in your brain as does beautiful sea-blue Cavansite. Endorphins are natural antidepressants that greatly enhance your feel-good factor.

Yellow or Golden Calcite instils a quiet joy deep within and facilitates the joy of spiritual connection as does Stellar Beam Calcite and Chrysoprase. Pink Chalcedony and Mangano Calcite increase joy in your heart. If you want to enjoy life to the fullest, wear Emeralds or carry Green Tourmaline.

Optimism

Having an optimistic outlook on life adds to your joy, and wearing Citrine overcomes innate pessimism and instils hope and optimism. As pessimism only flourishes when you feel low in energy, wear Carnelian, Citrine or Topaz to raise your energy levels and create a positive outlook on life. The stones transform negativity into joy.

Feeling positive

Whenever you need to feel particularly positive, connect to Iron Pyrite. The strength in this stone both motivates and activates you to move into joy.

Chakra support system: Place yellow crystals over your solar plexus, and green or pink stones over your heart. If you want to connect to the joy of creativity, add an orange stone to your sacral chakra.

Suggested exercises: Gratitude and blessings page 140, Inner-wealth ritual page 168.

Section 5
The Prosperity Stones
Compendium

The colour of abundance

A correspondence between different coloured stones and prosperity is an ancient concept as is that of the chakras and colour (see page 50). Gold and golden stones have long been associated with wealth, creativity and the sun that makes things grow, and green stones with the abundance of nature and new growth. Traditionally, gold stones enhance our self-esteem and the feeling that we deserve unlimited abundance, while many red stones are associated with the planet Mars, which symbolises motivation, ambition and the drive to move forward in life plus the willpower to manifest our desires.

Some of the stones in the A–Z Directory can be found in myriad forms and colours but the basic energy of the stone remains the same although it may be enhanced by additional properties specific to the variety or colour.

Choose four or five of the stones in this short compendium for your abundance pack.

Agate

Grounding energy and stabilising matter, Agate assists in bringing your prosperity into concrete manifestation. Most Agates act slowly to bring about practical solutions and to help you attune to your core stability. If you need assistance in fully accepting yourself, Agate is your stone. It increases your confidence and your ability to concentrate, facilitating finding inner security.

Tree Agate acts slowly to draw material success into your life. With its powerful connection to living things, this is the stone for success in cultivating your inner wealth and for ethically using natural resources. A stone of perseverance, it helps you to feel safe in the most challenging of circumstances.

Dendritic Agate can be similar to Tree Agate in appearance, and is known as the stone of plenitude as it brings abundance to all areas of your life but especially to businesses that are connected to nature and natural resources.

Moss Agate also has a profound connection to nature and all that grows. As a birthing crystal, it is extremely useful whenever you are starting a new venture or making a new beginning in your life. It is the perfect stone if you have lost hope as it promotes trying one more time and gives you insight into why your efforts have not been successful so far, so that you can amend your plans and achieve success.

Ammolite

The Feng Shui prosperity stone (see page 147), Ammolite offers both the power of attraction and personal empowerment. It stimulates your creativity and stamina, teaching you that perseverance pays off. It is a great stone to keep in the home to promote well-being and in business premises to ensure success. This stone works well with the base chakra to activate your survival instincts and with the third eye to promote mental clarity and insight. It can also be magnetised to bring a project to fruition. Ammonite can be substituted.

Ancestralite

Removing ingrained ancestral beliefs and poverty consciousness carried through ancestral life, Ancestralite attunes the ancestral line to the abundant universe. It assists lineage breakers to cut with the past, so that toxic karmas and attitudes do not carry forward into future generations. It literally says: "The buck stops here. It's up to you so get on with it. Now!"

Aventurine

Used by gamblers as a lucky talisman, Aventurine is an excellent gratitude stone as it helps you to value what you already have. It overcomes the feeling of lack that so often underlies poverty consciousness, helping you to look forward with joyous expectation and providing support if you are going outside your comfort zone. If you need to take a long hard look at yourself or your plans, this stone assists. Aventurine helps to turn a situation around and assists you to spot business opportunities that enrich your life in unexpected ways. It increases confidence and brings out leadership qualities. If you need encouragement to persevere or have a difficult decision to make, keep an Aventurine palmstone in your pocket. Tape it over your kidneys to overcome fear.

Calcite

Excellent for drawing prosperity into your home. A motivational stone, Calcite gives you the courage to act and to be yourself. It releases limiting beliefs and mental conditioning and forms a bridge between an idea and its coming to fruition.

Green Calcite releases poverty consciousness and the belief that you don't deserve anything. It helps you to move out of your comfort zone.

White or Clear Calcite is a stone of new beginnings that facilitates major change.

Pink Mangano Calcite strengthens self-acceptance and self-worth, and increases the capacity for unconditional love, especially for yourself.

If your willpower needs strengthening, **Red or Yellow Calcite** assists.

Carnelian

Carnelian imbues a person who is set on a difficult course of action with courage, ensuring that a positive end is reached. A crystal of creativity, Carnelian has great vitality and is a powerful energizer, especially for the lower chakras. A stone of regeneration, it assists in making positive life choices and in turning daydreams into reality. If you lack motivation or suffer from mental lethargy, this is the stone for you. Carnelian transmutes anger or a sense of victimhood into empowerment and the drive to get things moving. Traditionally it should be placed in the porch or doorway of a house to invite prosperity to enter your home.

Chalcedony

Chalcedony is a gentle nurturing stone that fosters generosity and benevolence. It releases toxic thoughts.

Blue Chalcedony promotes creativity and promulgation of new ideas. It helps you to adjust optimistically to new situations and make the best of them.

Energetic **Red Chalcedony** endows you with confidence and persistence when striving to reach your goals. This stone is most useful for devising strategies that manifest your dreams.

Chrysoprase

Promotes hope and helps to draw out your creativity so that you fully express all your talents. It instils a deep sense of emotional security and encourages you to be independent where needed. This stone teaches that cooperation is far more enriching than competition. Wear it to attract like-minded people who enjoy sharing mutual interests and exploring all the joys that life has to offer.

Cinnabar

Placed in a cashbox, Cinnabar draws in wealth and enables you to hold on to what you have. This is a stone for successful financial dealings.

Caution: Cinnabar is a toxic stone, use tumbled, handle it with care and wash hands after use.

Citrine

Traditionally known as 'the Merchant Stone', Citrine is prized for its prosperity-enhancing properties. Keep a Citrine in your purse or in a cash box – or the wealth corner of your home – to attract money. Keep it in your pocket if you are seeking success. Paradoxically, this stone encourages both generosity and accumulation of wealth. Helping you to freely share joy and abundance and expand your heart, it teaches that what you give away returns multiplied fourfold and that generosity of spirit is both a precious gift and a powerful generator of wealth on all levels. Bright yellow-orange 'Citrine' is often artificially formed by heat-treatment of Amethyst or Smoky Quartz. Natural Citrine tends to be paler or smokier than the bright yellow or chestnut brown of the artificially heat-amended crystal but all work equally well in prosperity rituals and layouts.

Eye of the Storm (Judy's Jasper)

This incredibly calming stone helps you to feel cool, centred and confident during periods of upheaval and necessary change. Reminding you that the bigger picture is fluid and ever changing depending on actions taken, Eye of the Storm reprograms a sense of lack into abundance. For people who feel that the world owes them a living, it shows the value of fair reward. For those with no sense of entitlement, it offers a fundamental sense of worth.

Garnet

Square-cut Garnets are said to ensure success in business. This is an excellent stone to keep with you in a challenging situation that is, seemingly, hopeless. It strengthens your survival instinct, instils fortitude and turns a crisis into an opportunity. Garnet assists you to release outdated ideas and plan for the future.

Almandine Garnet supports you in taking time out for yourself.

Andradite Garnet stimulates your creativity and instils courage.

Grossular Garnet is an excellent stone for manifestation. This crystal teaches how to go with the flow and inspires you to service towards your fellow human beings.

Uvarovite Garnet promotes your individuality without falling into the trap of egocentricity. It helps you to value solitude.

Goldstone

Instilling in the wearer a positive attitude and unshakeable self-confidence, Goldstone supports courage to try something new and enhances energy levels. You experience the pleasure of being fully alive and inwardly wealthy.

Iron Pyrite

Also known as 'Fools Gold', Iron Pyrite is an exceptionally strong and fast-acting 'macho' stone that gets things moving. If you need help to see what lies beneath a façade, call on Iron Pyrite, and also if you want to tap into your own potential or to boost your self-confidence. It is useful in business as it energizes projects – although it can be too strong if there are 'macho men' around. It works best for women and gentle men, instilling stamina and insight within a spirit of cooperation. Use it as a paperweight on a desk to keep ideas flowing. An Iron Pyrite-in-Quartz stone is an energetic combination for manifestation.

Jade

The ultimate attractor of good luck and enduring friendship. Jade assists you to be grateful for what you have, and to recognise that true riches are not found in the bank but rather within your own self. If you have issues around money whether they are poverty consciousness or regarding it almost as a god, Jade assists in regarding money positively, valuing what you have and using it wisely. This stone helps you to think laterally to bring out hidden riches – or to take a lucky gamble. Releasing ingrained core beliefs and changing your attitude, Jade helps you be yourself. If you seek partners for new ventures, it finds people with integrity and foresight.

Lapis Lazuli

Instilling self-awareness and serenity, Lapis Lazuli teaches you the power of the spoken word and heightens your creativity. This stone is a thought amplifier that teaches the value of active listening.

Malachite

Helps you to explore your innermost being. Use it for problem solving and to find your path forward. An intense stone that encourages risk-taking and brings about transformation, if you need to break old patterns Malachite assists. It is a supportive stone for friendship but helps you to break outgrown ties.

Caution: Malachite is a toxic stone. Use in its tumbled form and wash hands after handling.

Moonstone

A stone of new beginnings and intuitive understanding, Moonstone helps you work with cycles and flows tuning into exactly the right moment for action or non-action. This stone draws out old emotional patterning that restricts you but it can also make you overly emotional at full moon.

Black Moonstone is a stone of discernment and protection, separating illusion from reality, and regulating emotional highs and lows. It assists in knowing exactly the right moment to act, or to see hidden agendas.

Blue Moonstone enables you to keep a foot in both worlds: the spiritual and material.

Peridot

A stone of financial and spiritual abundance, Peridot releases the negative beliefs and toxic thought patterns and feelings that underlie poverty consciousness and instils confidence in your own abilities. It assists you to see the gifts in your past, including mistakes that can be turned into learning experiences. It brings about change, especially ones based on recognition of your own inner resources. Peridot helps you to leave behind old habits such as spending too much or being miserly. It assists you to put out to the universe the message that you are ready to accept abundance right now.

Quartz
See page 32 for the shapes of Quartz that best manifest abundance.

Ruby
Long prized for its ability to attract – and retain – wealth. Strengthening motivation and instilling passion for life, Ruby helps you to set realistic goals and offers the courage to bring your dreams to fruition. If you want to enhance your individuality while at the same time retaining your connection to those around you, wear Ruby in Zoisite (Anyolite).

Sapphire
Brings an influx of prosperity into your life which can be money or other resources.

Black Sapphire enhances your employment prospects or ability to retain your job in challenging times.

Pink Sapphire is a magnet that draws into your life everything you need for growth and self-development.

Yellow Sapphire in your cashbox is said to keep the money rolling in.

Tiger's Eye

Long seen as a fortunate stone that protects your resources, Tiger's Eye enhances your ability to make money, and imbues the wearer with the ability to accomplish goals. It brings out your assertion skills and is an excellent stone if you want to make wise use of your own power and draw on inner resources. It assists in recognising skills and talents and facilitates change, creating opportunities. If you have been suffering from blocked creativity, Tiger's Eye releases this. A useful stone for gathering together disparate pieces of information and synthesising them into a coherent whole, it also assists in separating what you think you want from what you really need and recognising the right moment for action. Distinguishing wishful thinking from attainable possibilities, it strengthens your self-confidence and commitment.

Topaz

Wearing zingy Topaz makes you feel rich in all ways. Helping you to tap into your inner riches, it assists with achieving your goals and finding solutions to problems. Instilling trust in the universe, it helps you to *be* rather than *do*. This vibrant crystal is imbued with joy, generosity and abundance. Helping you to be philanthropic and generous, it assists you to share your resources and to spread happiness. Excellent for all creative pursuits, Topaz boosts your confidence and encourages lateral thinking when solving problems.

Blue Topaz helps you to live with integrity in accordance with your own values and aspirations. If you have strayed from your own truth, it gently points the way back.

Golden (Imperial) Topaz is one of the most energetic forms of Topaz. Acting like a battery, it recharges your energies and your optimism. It assists in recognising your own abilities and enhances your charisma. If you have great plans, Topaz is the perfect companion to facilitate manifesting them.

Gentle **Pink Topaz** dissolves any resistance you may have to letting go of old patterns.

Tourmaline

Removes victim consciousness and instils self-confidence in its place.

Indicolite (Blue) Tourmaline is particularly useful for sharing your inner resources with others in an act of service and for living in harmony with the environment.

Pink Tourmaline attracts a wealth of love.

Purple Tourmaline sweeps away illusions and helps you to have realistic dreams.

Encouraging service to others, **Paraiba Tourmaline** promotes forgiveness and removes self-defeating patterns.

Turquoise

If you need a creative solution to problems, look to Turquoise. If you have a tendency to sabotage yourself just when you're achieving all you've dreamed of, wear Turquoise and all is well. This gentle stone quietly strengthens your belief in yourself and projects it forward into the future.

Section 6

A–Z Crystal Directory

Choose one or two crystals from a list (see page 3).
Note: Certain crystals contain potentially toxic substances. If
(caution toxic) appears in the text, use the stone in tumbled form
whenever possible and wash your hands after touching the stone.

– A –

Abandonment, heal: Amazonite, Aventurine, Carnelian, Cassiterite, Chalcanthite, Chrysoprase, Dioptase, Eye of the Storm, Grape Chalcedony, Mangano Calcite, Morganite, Prairie Tanzanite, Quantum Quattro, Rhodonite, Rhodozaz, Rose Quartz, Ruby in Zoisite or Kyanite, Snowflake Obsidian, Tugtupite, Unakite, Uvarovite. *Chakra:* base, sacral, heart

Abundance: Amber, Ammolite, Aventurine, Citrine, Emerald, Emerald and Cherry Quartz, Eye of the Storm, Fire Agate, Garnet, Goldstone, Green Tourmaline, Jade, Magnetite, Moss Agate, Opal, Orange Calcite, Peridot, Pyrite, Quartz, Ruby, Rutilated Quartz, Shiva Shell, Smoky Quartz, Sodalite, Sunstone, Tiger's Eye, Turquoise, Yellow Sapphire. *Chakra:* All

Abuse: Apricot Quartz, Azeztulite with Morganite, Eilat Stone, Honey Opal, Lazurine, Lemurian Jade, Morganite, Pink Crackle Quartz, Proustite, Red Quartz, Septarian, Smoky Amethyst, Smoky Citrine, Xenotine. *Chakra:* base, sacral

Achievable dream or illusion: Carnelian, Charoite, Moonstone, Labradorite, Purple Tourmaline, Smoky Quartz. *Chakra:* third eye *(and see illusions)*

Alienation, overcome: Amethyst, Amphibole Quartz, Apatite, Bustamite with Sugilite, Champagne Aura Quartz, Charoite, Eye of the Storm, Gaia Stone, Kiwi Jasper, Lapis Lazuli, Muscovite, Rhodochrosite. *Chakra:* earth star, solar plexus, soma

Alta major chakra: Afghanite, African Jade (Budd Stone), Amethyst Aura Quartz, Angelinite, Angel's Wing Calcite,

Anandalite, Andara Glass, Apatite, Auralite 23, Aurichalcite, Azeztulite, Black Amber, Black Moonstone, Blue Moonstone, Brandenberg Amethyst, Crystal Cap Amethyst, Diaspore (Zultanite), Emerald, Ethiopian Opal, Eye of the Storm (Judy's Jasper), Fire and Ice Quartz, Fluorapatite, Garnet in Pyroxene, Golden Healer, Golden Herkimer Diamond, Graphic Smoky Quartz, Green Ridge Quartz, Holly Agate, Kyanite, Petalite, Phenacite, Preseli Bluestone, Rainbow Covellite, Rainbow Mayanite, Red Agate, Red Amethyst, Rosophia. *Chakra:* past life, alta major, base

> **balance and align:** Anandalite, Brandenberg Amethyst, Crystal Cap Amethyst, Green Ridge Quartz, Preseli Bluestone. Rub gently on soma chakra with Angel's Wing Calcite or Herkimer Diamond.
>
> **spin too rapid/stuck open:** African Jade (Budd Stone), Auralite 23, Black Moonstone, Calcite, Eye of the Storm, Flint, Golden Healer, Graphic Smoky Quartz
>
> **spin too sluggish/stuck closed:** Blue Moonstone, Diaspore, Ethiopian Opal, Herkimer Diamond, Quartz, Red Agate

Ancestral attachment/myths/stories carried in the genes: Anandalite, Ancestralite, Brandenberg Amethyst, Celtic Quartz, Cradle of Life (Humankind), Datolite, Fairy Quartz, Freedom Stone, Lakelandite, Lemurian Seed, Preseli Bluestone, Rainforest Jasper, Seftonite, Smoky Elestial, Spirit Quartz. *Chakra:* soma, causal vortex, solar plexus

Ancestral healer: Ammolite, Ammonite, Anandalite,

Ancestral healer (large crystal with a distinctive flat pathway running up the crystal from bottom to top), Ancestralite, Brandenberg Amethyst, Celtic Chevron Quartz, Chrysotile, Cradle of Life (Humankind), Dumortierite, Elestial Quartz, Fairy Quartz, Freedom Stone, Kambaba Jasper, Lakelandite, Mother and child formation (a large crystal to which is attached a smaller crystal or crystals that appears to be enfolded), Petrified Wood, Preseli Bluestone, Seftonite, Smithsonite, Smoky Elestial, Spirit Quartz, Stromatolite, Turritella Agate, Trigonic Quartz, Turritella Agate, Wind Fossil Agate. *Chakra:* past life, causal vortex

Ancestral issues: Ancestralite, Anthrophyllite, Blue Holly Agate, Brandenberg Amethyst, Bumble Bee Jasper *(caution toxic)*, Candle Quartz, Catlinite, Datolite, Eclipse Stone, Fairy Quartz, Icicle Calcite, Ilmenite, Jade, Kambaba Jasper, Lakelandite, Lemurian Aquitane Calcite, Mohawkite, Morganite, Peanut Wood, Petrified Wood, Porphyrite, Prasiolite, Preseli Bluestone, Preseli Companion, Rainbow Mayanite, Rainforest Jasper, Shaman Quartz, Smoky Elestial Quartz, Spirit Quartz, Star Stone, Starseed, Stromatolite. *Chakra:* soul star, past life, alta major, causal vortex, higher heart, earth star and Gaia gateway

Anchoring stones: Black Tourmaline, Chrysanthemum Stone, Flint, Hematite, Smoky Elestial Quartz, Smoky Quartz. *Chakra:* dantien, base, earth star, Gaia gateway

Anger, ameliorate: Blue Apatite, Blue Lace Agate, Cinnabar in Jasper *(caution toxic)*, Ethiopian Opal, Eye of the Storm, Howlite, Lapis Lace, Muscovite, Nzuri Moyo, Peridot, Pink Carnelian, Prairie Tanzanite, Rhodonite, Rose Quartz, Smoky Quartz. *Chakra:* base, sacral, dantien

Anxiety: Amethyst, Amethyst Aura Quartz, Eye of the Storm, Galaxyite, Khutnohorite, Kunzite, Kyanite, Lemurian Aquitane Calcite, Lemurian Gold Opal, Nzuri Moyo, Oceanite, Owyhee Blue Opal, Pyrite in Magnesite, Riebekite with Sugilite and Bustamite, Rose Quartz, Scolecite, Strawberry Quartz, Tanzanite, Thunder Egg, Tremolite, Tugtupite. *Chakra:* earth star, base

Apathy: Apatite, Carnelian, Citrine, Red Jasper. *Chakra:* base, sacral, dantien

Attract love: Green Aventurine, Mangano Calcite, Pink Tourmaline (Rubellite), Rose Quartz. *Chakra:* Heart

Attract money: Carnelian, Citrine, Garnet, Green Grossular Garnet, Green Tourmaline (Verdelite), Jet, Manifestation Quartz, Quartz Generator, Yellow Sapphire, *and see Abundance*

Autonomy: Candle Quartz, Carnelian, Cradle of Life (Humankind), Faden Quartz, Flint, Freedom Stone, Frondellite with Strengite, Pietersite, Pyrolusite, Pyrophyllite, Rhodolite Garnet, Ussingite. *Chakra:* dantien

– B –

Baggage, releasing emotional: Ajoite, Chrysotile in Serpentine, Cumberlandite, Eclipse Stone, Garnet in Quartz, Golden Healer Quartz, Graphic Smoky Quartz (Zebra Stone), Mount Shasta Opal, Rose Elestial Quartz, Tangerose, Tanzine Aura Quartz, Tremolite, Tugtupite, Wind Fossil Agate, Xenotine. *Chakra:* solar plexus, heart

Balance: Agate, bicoloured stones, Blue Moonstone, Gaia's Blood Flint, Lapis Lace, Merlinite, Onyx, Prairie Tanzanite, Sunset Sodalite. *Chakra:* dantien

Bargain, find: Aventurine

Base chakra: Amber, Azurite, Bastnasite, Black Obsidian, Black Opal, Black Tourmaline, Bloodstone, Candle Quartz, Carnelian, Chinese Red Quartz, Chrysocolla, Cinnabar in Jasper *(caution toxic)*, Citrine, Clinohumite, Cuprite, Dragon Stone, Eye of the Storm (Judy's Jasper), Fire Agate, Fulgarite, Gabbro, Garnet, Golden Topaz, Harlequin Quartz (Hematite in Quartz), Hematite, Kambaba Jasper, Keyiapo, Limonite, Obsidian, Pink Tourmaline, Poppy Jasper, Realgar and Orpiment, Red Amethyst, Red Calcite, Red Jasper, Red Zincite, Ruby, Serpentine, Serpentine in Obsidian, Shungite, Smoky Quartz, Sonora Sunrise, Spinel, Stromatolite, Tangerose, Triplite, Zircon

> **balance and align:** Anandalite, Celestobarite, Green Ridge Quartz, Hematite Quartz, Red Calcite, Red Coral, Ruby, Shiva Lingam

> **spin too rapid/stuck open:** Agate, Green Ridge Quartz, Mahogany Obsidian, Pink Tourmaline,

Smoky Quartz, Triplite in matrix

spin too sluggish/stuck closed: Fire Agate, Hematite, Kundalini Quartz, Red Calcite, Serpentine, Sonora Sunrise, Triplite

Beliefs that no longer serve, release: Ancestralite, Cradle of Life (Humankind), Fluorite, Freedom Stone, Geothite, Lakelandite. *Chakra:* causal vortex, past life, third eye

Believe you deserve it: Green Calcite. *Chakra:* heart

Bigger picture: Eye of the Storm, Shiva Eye. *Chakra:* third eye

Blessings: Amethyst, Lapis Lace, Mookaite, Temple Calcite

Blockages, remove: Black Obsidian, Black Tourmaline, Hematite, Iron Pyrite, Mahogany Obsidian, Red Jasper, Snowflake Obsidian, Red Zincite. *Chakra:* base

Boundaries: Agate, Aventurine, Calcite, Labradorite, Lavender Jade, Mohawkite, Tantalite. *Chakra:* base, sacral, dantien, higher heart

Bring a request to fruition: Citrine, Green Calcite, Manifestation crystal, *and see Abundance*

Bringing a dream into being: Black Moonstone, Calcite, Carnelian, Flint, Hematite, Heulandite, Iron Pyrite, Jade, Manifestation Quartz, Quartz Generator, Red Chalcedony, Ruby, Smoky Quartz. *Chakra:* heart

Budgeting: Cinnabar *(caution toxic)*, Citrine, Green Spinel, Hematite, Peridot, *and see Managing your money*

Burn-out, overcome: Crackled Fire Agate, Marcasite, Poppy Jasper, Quantum Quattro, Que Sera, Red Zincite, Strawberry Lemurian Seed. *Chakra:* base, dantien

– C –

Calming emotions: Amethyst, Chrysoprase, Eye of the Storm, Mount Shasta Opal, Oceanite, Rose Quartz, Tugtupite. *Chakra: heart, and see specific emotional entries*

Calming fear: Amethyst, Arsenopyrite, Eilat Stone, Eye of the Storm, Graphic Smoky Quartz (Zebra Stone), Guardian Stone, Khutnohorite, Oceanite, Rose Quartz, Scolecite, Tangerose, Thunder Egg. *Chakra: sacral, heart*

Car: Aventurine, Black Calcite, Blue Calcite, Brown Calcite, Calcite, Chrysoprase, Dendritic Agate, Indicolite, Lapis Lazuli, Mangano Calcite, Moss Agate, Red Calcite, Ruby, Smoky Quartz, Tiger's Eye

Career: Bloodstone, Chrysoprase, Citrine, Fluorite, Green Aventurine, Hematite, Iron Pyrite, Lapis Lazuli, Malachite, Obsidian

Causal vortex chakra: Ajoite, Apatite, Azeztulite, Banded White Agate, Black or Blue Moonstone, Blue Kyanite, Brandenberg Amethyst, Chrysotile, Cobalto Calcite, Cryolite, Crystalline Blue Kyanite, Diamond, Diaspore (Zultanite), Fluorapatite, Herderite, Petalite, Phenacite, Rainbow Moonstone, Scolecite, Sugilite, Tanzanite

> **balance and align:** Anandalite, Brandenberg Amethyst, Chrysotile, Crystalline Blue Kyanite, Fluorapatite, Phenacite, Scolecite, Smoky Elestial Quartz
>
> **spin too rapid/stuck open:** Black Moonstone, Cobalto Calcite, Diaspore, Scolecite with Natrolite
>
> **spin too sluggish/stuck closed:** Ajoite, Blue

Moonstone, Herderite, Petalite, Tanzanite

Centring: Agate, Amethyst, Aragonite, Bloodstone, Blue Euclase, Calcite, Celestobarite, Chrysanthemum Stone, Eye of the Storm, Flint, Fossilised Wood, Garnet, Grape Chalcedony, Hematite, Kunzite, Lapis Lace, Obsidian, Onyx, Peanut Wood, Prairie Tanzanite, Quartz, Red Jasper, Ruby, Sardonyx, Shiva Lingam, Shungite, Smoky Quartz, Tourmalinated Quartz. *Chakra:* Gaia gateway, earth star, base, dantien

Childhood, difficult: Cassiterite, Fenster Quartz, Pink Carnelian, Red Phantom Quartz, Shiva Lingam, Tugtupite, Tugtupite with Nuummite, Voegesite, Youngite. *Chakra:* heart, solar plexus

Chronic anxiety: Amethyst, Chrysocolla, Eye of the Storm, Grape Chalcedony, Kunzite, Lapis Lace, Prairie Tanzanite. *Chakra:* heart

Clarity, promote: Adamite, Amazez, Ammolite, Auralite 23, Blue Moonstone, Blue Quartz, Chinese Chromium Quartz, Chinese Red Quartz, Datolite, Dumortierite, Eye of the Storm (Judy's Jasper), Fluorite, Green Ridge Quartz, Holly Agate, Lemurian Seed, Leopardskin Jasper, Limonite, Marcasite, Morion, Pearl Spa Dolomite, Purpurite, Rainforest Jasper, Realgar and Orpiment *(caution toxic)*, Scapolite, Seriphos Quartz, Silver Leaf Jasper, Smoky Candle Quartz, Super 7, Tangerine Sun Aura Quartz, Tugtupite. *Chakra:* third eye, alta major, crown

Clearing grids: Flint, Hematite, Shungite, Smoky Elestial Quartz, Smoky Quartz, *and see Toxic thoughts and emotions*

Codependency, breakaway: Amazez, Amethyst Aura Quartz, Black Amber, Bytownite, Dumortierite, Fenster Quartz, Iolite, Iolite and Sunstone, Jasper, Quantum Quattro, Rose Quartz, Sichuan Quartz, Vera Cruz Amethyst, Zenotine. *Chakra:* base, dantien, causal vortex

Compassion for oneself and others: Ajoite, Amazez, Brandenberg Amethyst, Cobalto Calcite, Erythrite, Gaia Stone, Geothite, Golden Healer, Green Diopside, Green Ridge Quartz, Greenlandite, Mangano Vesuvianite, Paraiba Tourmaline, Rhodolite Garnet, Shaman Quartz, Smoky Cathedral Quartz, Starseed Quartz, Tangerose, Tanzanite, Tugtupite. *Chakra:* heart seed

Compulsive or obsessive thoughts: Ammolite, Auralite 23, Azurite, Barite, Bytownite, K2, Kiwi Jasper, Optical Calcite, Rhomboid Selenite, Scolecite, Spirit Quartz, Tantalite. *Chakra:* third eye, crown

Confidence: Carnelian, Citrine, Iron Pyrite, Orange Calcite, Red Jasper, Sunstone

Control freak: Chrysotile, Ice Quartz, Lazulite, Lemurian Aquitane Calcite, Spider Web Obsidian. *Chakra:* dantien

Creative solutions: Sunset Sodalite, *and see Creativity*

Creative success: Andradite Garnet, Aventurine, Dendritic Agate, Garnet, Iolite-Sunstone, Lapis Lazuli, Manifestation Quartz, Quartz Generator, Tiger's Eye

Creativity, increase: Chinese Writing Stone, Citrine, Graphic Smoky Quartz, Iolite and Sunstone, Rooster Booster (Amphibole in Quartz)

Critical thoughts: *see Inner Critic*

Crown chakra: Afghanite, Amethyst, Amphibole Quartz,

Angelite, Angel's Wing Calcite, Arfvedsonite, Auralite 23, Brandenberg Amethyst, Brookite, Celestial Quartz, Citrine, Clear Tourmaline, Diaspore (Zultanite), Golden Beryl, Golden Healer, Green Ridge Quartz, Herderite, Heulandite, Larimar, Lepidolite, Moldavite, Natrolite, Novaculite, Petalite, Phenacite, Purple Jasper, Purple Sapphire, Quartz, Rosophia, Satyamani and Satyaloka Quartz, Scolecite, Selenite, Serpentine, Sugilite, Titanite (Sphene), Trigonic, White Calcite, White Topaz

> **balance and align:** Amethyst, Anandalite, Auralite 23, Brandenberg Amethyst, Phenacite, Selenite, Sugilite
> **spin too rapid/stuck open:** Amethyst, Amphibole Quartz, Larimar, Petalite, Serpentine, White Calcite
> **spin too sluggish/stuck closed:** Moldavite, Phenacite, Rosophia, Selenite

Curses, break ancestral: Black Amber, Freedom Stone, Isua, Nuummite, Preseli Bluestone, Purpurite, Quantum Quattro, Shattuckite, Star Stone, Stibnite *(caution toxic)*, Tiger's Eye, Tourmalinated Quartz. *Chakra:* past life, throat, third eye, causal vortex

– D –

Dantien: Amber, Carnelian, Chinese Red Quartz, Empowerite, Eye of the Storm, Fire Agate, Fire Opal, Golden Herkimer, Green Ridge Quartz, Hematite, Hematoid Calcite, Kambaba Jasper, Madagascan Red Celestial Quartz, Moonstone, Orange River Quartz, Peanut Wood, Polychrome Jasper, Poppy Jasper, Red Amethyst, Red Jasper, Rhodozite, Rose or Ruby Aura Quartz, Rosophia, Stromatolite, Topaz

> **balance and align:** Empowerite, Eye of the Storm, Green Ridge Quartz, Poppy Jasper
>
> **spin too rapid/stuck open:** Peanut Wood, Polychrome Jasper, Stromatolite
>
> **spin too sluggish/stuck closed:** Fire Agate, Fire Opal, Hematite, Madagascan Red Celestial Quartz, Poppy Jasper, Red Jasper

Debts, gain repayment: Amber, Blue Kyanite, Flint, Sapphire

Debts, recognise past life: Lemurian Seed, Nuummite, Purple Scapolite. *Chakra:* past life, solar plexus

Defensive walls, dismantle: Calcite Fairy Stone, Eye of the Storm

Despair: Novaculite, Pyrite in Quartz, Vera Cruz Amethyst. *Chakra:* heart

Despondency: Amethyst, Purpurite. *Chakra:* heart

Determination: Hematite, Picture Jasper, Rhyolite, Tiger Iron

Detoxify emotions: Black Amber, Golden Danburite,

Golden Healer, Rhodolite Garnet, Rhodonite, Seraphinite, Spirit Quartz. *Chakra:* solar plexus

Distress: Eye of the Storm, Lemurian Gold Opal, Owyhee Blue Opal, Tugtupite. *Chakra:* heart

Dreams, attain: Charoite, Labradorite, *and see page 196*

Dysfunctional patterns, dissolve: Alunite, Amazez, Arfvedsonite, Celadonite, Dumortierite, Fenster Quartz, Fluorite, Garnet in Quartz, Glendonite, Rainbow Covellite, Scheelite, Stellar Beam Calcite, Spider Web Obsidian. *Chakra:* crown

– E –

Earth star chakra: Agnitite™, Boji Stone, Brown Jasper, Celestobarite, Champagne Aura Quartz, Cuprite, Fire Agate, Flint, Gaia Flint, Galena *(caution toxic)*, Golden Herkimer, Graphic Smoky Quartz, Hematite, Lemurian Jade, Limonite, Madagascan Red Celestial Quartz, Mahogany Obsidian, Proustite, Red Amethyst, Rhodonite, Rhodozite, Rosophia, Smoky Elestial Quartz, Smoky Quartz, Thunder Egg, Tourmaline

   balance and align: Blue Flint, Brown-flash Anandalite, Green Ridge Quartz, Hematite, Smoky Elestial Quartz

   spin too rapid/stuck open: Flint, Graphic Smoky Quartz, Green Ridge Quartz, Smoky Quartz

   spin too sluggish/stuck closed: Golden Herkimer, Hematite, Red Amethyst, Rhodozite, Thunder Egg

Egotism: Bixbite, Hematoid Calcite, Lepidocrocite, Rathbunite™, Red Amethyst. *Chakra:* base, dantien

EMF pollution, protect against: Ajoite in Shattuckite, Amazonite, Amber, Andara Glass, Black Moonstone, Black Tourmaline, Blizzard Stone, Champagne Aura Quartz, Chlorite Quartz, Diamond, Flint, Fluorite, Gabbro, Galena *(caution toxic)*, Graphic Smoky Quartz, Hackmanite, Herkimer Diamond, Klinoptilolith, Kunzite, Lepidolite, Malachite, Marble, Morion, Native Copper, Orgonite, Phlogopite, Poppy Jasper, Quartz, Que Sera, Red Amethyst, Rose Quartz, Shieldite, Shungite, Smoky Elestial Quartz, Smoky Herkimer Diamond, Smoky

Quartz, Sodalite, Tantalite, Thunder Egg. *Chakra:* earth star, base. *Or place in environment or around house.*

Emotional abuse: Azeztulite with Morganite, Cobalto Calcite, Eilat Stone, Lazurine, Pink Crackle Quartz, Proustite, Tugtupite. *Chakra:* sacral, heart

Emotional alienation: Cassiterite

Emotional angst: Hemimorphite, Rhodonite

Emotional attachment: Brandenberg, Drusy Golden Healer, Hemimorphite, Pink Crackle Quartz, Rainbow Mayanite, Tinguaite

Emotional autonomy: Faden Quartz. *Chakra:* dantien

Emotional balance: Amblygonite, Dalmatian Stone, Eilat Stone

Emotional black hole: Ajoite, Cobalto Calcite, Quantum Quattro. *Chakra:* higher heart

Emotional blackmail: Tugtupite. *Chakra:* solar plexus

Emotional blockages: Aegirine, Botswana Agate, Bowenite (New Jade), Clinohumite, Cobalto Calcite, Eilat Stone, Green Ridge Quartz, Prehnite with Epidote, Pyrite and Sphalerite, Quantum Quattro, Rainbow Mayanite, Rhodozite, Tangerose, Tanzine Aura Quartz. *Chakra:* solar plexus

Emotional blockages from past lives: Aegirine, Ancestralite, Black Amber, Datolite, Dumortierite, Graphic Smoky Quartz (Zebra Stone), Prehnite with Epidote, Pyrite and Sphalerite, Quantum Quattro, Rhodozite, Rose Elestial Quartz, Serpentine in Obsidian. *Chakra:* past life

Emotional bondage: Ajoite. *Chakra:* solar plexus

Emotional burn-out: Cobalto Calcite, Golden Healer Quartz, Lilac Quartz. *Chakra:* heart

Emotional conditioning: Clevelandite, Drusy Golden Healer, Golden Healer Quartz. *Chakra:* solar plexus, third eye

Emotional debris: Ajoite, Pink Lemurian Seed, Rainbow Mayanite. *Chakra:* solar plexus

Emotional dependency: Cobalto Calcite. *Chakra:* base

Emotional dysfunction: Chinese Red Phantom Quartz, Fenster Quartz, Orange Kyanite. *Chakra:* higher heart

Emotional equilibrium: Adamite, Merlinite, Quantum Quattro, Rutile with Hematite, Shungite

Emotional exhaustion: Cinnabar in Jasper *(caution toxic)*, Lilac Quartz, Orange River Quartz, Prehnite with Epidote

Emotional healing: Garnet in Quartz, Mount Shasta Opal, Tugtupite, Xenotine

Emotional hooks, remove: Amblygonite, Drusy Golden Healer, Geothite, Golden Danburite, Klinoptilolith, Novaculite, Nunderite, Nuummite, Orange Kyanite, Pyromorphite, Rainbow Mayanite, Tantalite, Tugtupite. *Chakra:* solar plexus

Emotional manipulation: Pink Lemurian Seed, Tantalite. *Chakra:* sacral, solar plexus, third eye

Emotional maturation: Alexandrite, Cobalto Calcite

Emotional negative, destructive attachments: Ajoite, Drusy Golden Healer, Ilmenite, Pink Lemurian Seed, Rainbow Mayanite, Tantalite, Tinguaite. *Chakra:* base, solar plexus

Emotional pain after separation: Aegirine, Eilat Stone, Tugtupite. *Chakra:* higher heart

Emotional patterns: Arfvedsonite, Brandenberg Amethyst, Celadonite, Fenster Quartz, Rainbow Covellite, Scheelite. *Chakra:* solar plexus, base

Emotional recovery: Empowerite, Eye of the Storm, Lilac Quartz. *Chakra:* higher heart

Emotional release: Axinite, Cobalto Calcite, Scheelite. *Chakra:* solar plexus, base, sacral

Emotional, reveal underlying causes of distress: Eye of the Storm, Gaia Stone, Lemurian Gold Opal, Obsidian, Rainbow Obsidian, Richterite, Riebekite with Sugilite and Bustamite, Smoky Amethyst, Snowflake Obsidian, Spider Web Obsidian. *Chakra:* solar plexus, past life

Emotional security: Eye of the Storm, Mangano Vesuvianite, Oceanite, Tugtupite. *Chakra:* base, dantien, solar plexus

Emotional shock: Amethyst, Kunzite, Tantalite, Tugtupite. *Chakra:* heart

Emotional shutdown, release: Ice Quartz, *and see Heart chakra*

Emotional strength: Brazilianite, Mohawkite, Picrolite, Tree Agate. *Chakra:* heart

Emotional stress, dissolve: Cobalto Calcite, Eye of the Storm, Icicle Calcite, Shungite, Tugtupite. *Chakra:* solar plexus

Emotional tension: Strawberry Quartz. *Chakra:* solar plexus

Emotional toxicity: Ajoite, Arsenopyrite, Banded Agate,

Champagne Aura Quartz, Drusy Danburite with Chlorite, Valentinite and Stibnite *(caution toxic)*

Emotional trauma: Ajoite, Blue Euclase, Cobalto Calcite, Empowerite, Epidote, Eye of the Storm, Gaia Stone, Grape Chalcedony, Graphic Smoky Quartz (Zebra Stone), Holly Agate, Mangano Vesuvianite, Orange River Quartz, Prairie Tanzanite, Richterite, Tantalite, Tugtupite, Victorite. *Chakra:* solar plexus

Emotional turmoil: Cobalto Calcite, Desert Rose. *Chakra:* base

Emotional wounds, heal: Ajoite, Bustamite, Cassiterite, Cobalto Calcite, Eilat Stone, Gaia Stone, Macedonian Opal, Mookite Jasper, Orange River Quartz, Piemontite, Rathbunite™, Rhodonite, Rose Quartz, Shungite, Xenotine. *Chakra:* higher heart

Emotions, frozen feelings: Clevelandite, Diopside, Eilat Stone, Ice Quartz, Scolecite. *Chakra:* solar plexus, heart, heart seed, higher heart

Emotions, restore trust: Clevelandite, Faden Quartz, Xenotine

Emotions, revitalize: Orange River Quartz, Vivianite

Empty nest syndrome: Gaia's Blood Flint, Menalite, Moonstone. *Chakra:* sacral

Endorphins: Citrine, Danburite, Kunzite, Porcelain Jasper, Red Jasper, *and see Joy bringers*

Environmentally friendly solutions: Ametrine, Dendritic Agate, Indicolite, Jade, Moss Agate, Smoky Quartz. *Chakra:* Gaia gateway, earth star, base

Express how you feel: Blue Lace Agate. *Chakra:* throat

– F –

Fear of expansion, overcome: Amethyst, Auralite 23, Kammerite, Moqui Marbles *(make essence by indirect method)*, Sunstone-and-Iolite

Fear of failure: Avalonite, Elestial Quartz

Fear of responsibility: Brazilianite, Hemimorphite, Ocean Jasper, Paraiba Tourmaline, Quantum Quattro

Fear, overcome: Aventurine, Eye of the Storm, Jasper

Feeling positive: Carnelian, Iron Pyrite, Pinolith, Red Jasper

Financial decisions: Amethyst, Tiger's Eye, *and see Managing your money*

Finding the right job: Black or Dark Blue Sapphire, Cinnabar *(caution toxic)*, Citrine, Golden Tiger's Eye, Holey Stone, Iron Pyrite, Jet, Magnetite, Manifestation Quartz, Moss Agate, Plume Agate, Quartz Generator, Tiger's Eye, Tree or other Agate

Forgiveness: Mangano Calcite, Paraiba Tourmaline, Peridot, Rose Quartz. *Chakra:* heart

Friendship: Agate, Barite, Blue Lace Agate, Carnelian, Emerald, Hematite, Jade, Lapis Lazuli, Rhodonite, Rose Quartz, Snowflake Obsidian, Unakite

Frustration, overcome: Chinese Red Quartz, Lapis Lace, Poppy Jasper, Pyrite in Magnesite, Rooster Tail Quartz. *Chakra:* base, dantien

– G –

Gaia gateway chakra: Apache Tear, Basalt, Bastnasite, Black Actinolite, Black Calcite, Black Flint, Black Kyanite, Black Obsidian, Black Petalite, Black Spinel, Black Spot Herkimer Diamond, Day and Night Quartz, Fire and Ice, Jet, Master Shamanite, Mohawkite, Morion, Naturally Dark Smoky Quartz (not irradiated Nebula Stone), Nirvana Quartz, Nuummite, Petalite, Preseli Bluestone, Sardonyx, Shungite, Smoky Elestial Quartz, Snowflake Obsidian, Specular Hematite, Spider Web Obsidian, Stromatolite, Tektite, Tibetan Black Spot Quartz, Tourmalinated Quartz, Verdelite

> **balance and align:** Black Flint, Day and Night Quartz, Fire and Ice, Master Shamanite, Morion, Shungite, Tourmalinated Quartz, Verdelite

> **spin too rapid/stuck open:** Apache Tear, Basalt, Black Flint, Black Kyanite, Master Shamanite, Sardonyx, Shungite

> **spin too sluggish/stuck closed:** Black Spot Herkimer Diamond, Nirvana Quartz, Preseli Bluestone, Shungite, Specular Hematite, Tektite, Tibetan Black Spot Quartz

Generosity: Amethyst, Aragonite, Bumble Bee Jasper *(caution toxic)*, Cassiterite, Chalcedony, Chrysoberyl, Citrine, Diamond, Emerald, Euclase, Imperial Topaz, Lapis Lazuli, Mookaite Jasper, Rhodonite, Sapphire, Sunstone. *Chakra:* heart

Geopathic stress: Amazonite, Amethyst, Black

Tourmaline, Brown Jasper, Champagne Aura Quartz, Chlorite Quartz, Eye of the Storm, Flint, Gabbro, Granite, Graphic Smoky Quartz, Ironstone, Kunzite, Labradorite, Marble, Orgonite, Preseli Bluestone, Pyrite and Sphalerite, Quartz, Riebekite with Sugilite and Bustamite, Selenite, Shieldite, Shungite, Smoky Amethyst, Smoky Elestial, Smoky Quartz, Sodalite, Strummer Jasper, Tantalite, Tektite, Thunder Egg. *Chakra:* earth star. Or disperse around corners of house.

Gratitude: Apatite, Green Apatite, Green Aventurine, Hiddenite, Larimar, Pietersite, Pink Sapphire, Rose Quartz, Selenite, Sodalite, Tiger's Eye

Grounding: Ajo Quartz, Amphibole, Aztee, Banded Agate, Basalt, Blue Aragonite, Boji Stones, Bronzite, Brown Jasper, Bustamite, Calcite Fairy Stone, Champagne Aura Quartz, Chlorite Quartz, Cloudy Quartz, Dalmatian Stone, Empowerite, Fire Agate, Flint, Gabbro, Granite, Healer's Gold, Hematite, Hematoid Calcite, Herkimer Diamond, Honey Phantom Quartz, Kambaba Jasper, Keyiapo, Lazulite, Lemurian Jade, Lemurian Seed, Leopardskin Serpentine, Libyan Gold Tektite, Limonite, Luxullianite, Marcasite, Merlinite, Mohawkite, Novaculite, Nunderite, Peanut Wood, Pearl Spa Dolomite, Petrified Wood, Poppy Jasper, Preseli Bluestone, Purpurite, Pyrite in Magnesite, Quantum Quattro, Red Jasper, Rutile with Hematite, Schalenblende, Serpentine in Obsidian, Smoky Elestial Quartz, Smoky Herkimer, Smoky Quartz, Sodalite, Steatite, Stromatolite. *Chakra:* base, earth star, dantien

– H –

Heart chakra: Apophyllite, Aventurine, Chrysocolla, Chrysoprase, Cobalto Calcite, Danburite, Eudialyte, Gaia Stone, Green Jasper, Green Quartz, Green Sapphire, Green Siberian Quartz, Green Tourmaline, Hematite Quartz, Herkimer Diamond, Jade, Jadeite, Kunzite, Lavender Quartz, Lepidolite, Malachite, Morganite, Muscovite, Pink Danburite, Pink Petalite, Pink Tourmaline, Pyroxmangite, Red Calcite, Rhodochrosite, Rhodonite, Rhodozaz, Rose Quartz, Rubellite Tourmaline, Ruby, Ruby Lavender Quartz, Tugtupite, Variscite, Watermelon Tourmaline

    balance and align: Anandalite, Cobalto Calcite, Kunzite, Mangano Calcite, Ruby Lavender Quartz, Watermelon Tourmaline

    clear heart chakra attachments: Banded Agate, Mangano Calcite

    open the three-chambered heart: Danburite, Lemurian Aquitane Calcite, Mangano Calcite, Pink Petalite, Pink Tourmaline, Rosophia, Tugtupite

    spin too rapid/stuck open: Green Tourmaline, Mangano Calcite, Quartz, Rose Quartz, Tugtupite

    spin too sluggish/stuck closed: Calcite, Chohua Jasper, Danburite, Erythrite, Honey Calcite, Lemurian Jade, Pink Lemurian Seed, Red Calcite, Rhodozaz, Rose Quartz, Strawberry Quartz, Tugtupite

Heart seed chakra: Ajo Blue Calcite, Ajoite, Azeztulite, Brandenberg Amethyst, Coral, Danburite, Dianite, Fire

Opal, Golden Healer, Green Ridge Quartz, Khutnohorite, Lemurian Calcite, Lilac Quartz, Macedonian Opal, Mangano Calcite, Merkabite Calcite, Pink Opal, Pyroxmangite, Rhodozaz, Roselite, Rosophia, Ruby Lavender Quartz, Scolecite, Spirit Quartz, Tugtupite, Violane

> **balance and align:** Danburite, Golden Healer, Golden Herkimer, Khutnohorite, Merkabite Calcite
>
> **spin too rapid/stuck open:** Ajo Blue Calcite, Khutnohorite, Macedonian Opal
>
> **spin too sluggish/stuck closed:** Fire Opal, Rhodozaz, Rosophia, Spirit Quartz

Helplessness: Actinolite Quartz, Adamite, Brazilianite, Bronzite, Carnelian, Clevelandite, Covellite, Dumortierite, Kakortokite, Mystic Topaz, Orange Calcite, Ocean Jasper, Paraiba Tourmaline, Pumice, Quantum Quattro, Red Jasper, Sunstone, Tree Agate. *Chakra:* earth star, base, sacral, dantien

Higher heart chakra: Ajo Blue Calcite, Amazonite, Anandalite (Aurora Quartz), Aqua Aura Quartz, Azeztulite, Bloodstone, Celestite, Danburite, Dioptase, Dream Quartz, Eye of the Storm, Fire and Ice Quartz, Gaia Stone, Green Siberian Quartz, Khutnohorite, Kunzite, Lavender Quartz, Lazurine, Lilac Quartz, Macedonian Opal, Mangano Calcite, Muscovite, Nirvana Quartz, Phenacite, Pink Crackle Quartz, Pink Lazurine, Pink or Lilac Danburite, Pink Petalite, Pyroxmangite, Quantum Quattro, Que Sera, Rainbow Mayanite, Raspberry Aura Quartz, Rhodozaz, Rose Elestial Quartz,

Rose Opal, Rose Quartz, Roselite, Rosophia, Ruby Aura Quartz, Ruby Lavender Quartz™, Spirit Quartz, Strawberry Lemurian, Strawberry Quartz, Tangerose, Tugtupite, Turquoise

> **balance and align:** Bloodstone, Eye of the Storm, Quantum Quattro, Que Sera, Tangerose
>
> **spin too rapid/stuck open:** Eye of the Storm, Mangano Calcite, Pink Petalite, Rose Elestial Quartz, Turquoise
>
> **spin too sluggish/stuck closed:** Quantum Quattro, Que Sera, Ruby Aura Quartz, Strawberry Lemurian

Holding on to money: *see Managing your money*

Holding space: Amazez, Anandalite, Black Amber, Brandenberg Amethyst, Calcite, Morganite, Selenite, Temple Calcite. *Chakra:* crown, soul star, stellar gateway. Place above head or at top or centre of grid.

Hope: Blue Quartz (Indicolite), Candle Quartz, Garnet, Moss Agate, Ruby in Zoisite or Kyanite, Sunstone. *Chakra:* heart

'Identified patient'/takes on the family pain or dis-ease: Diopside, Dioptase, Fenster Quartz, Gaia's Blood Flint, Grape Chalcedony, Green Zoisite, Kiwi Jasper, Mangano Calcite, Morganite, Pinolith, Polychrome Jasper, Prairie Tanzanite, Thulite. *Chakra:* navel

Ill-wishing, protection against: Actinolite, Amethyst, Black Tourmaline, Blue Chalcedony, Bronzite *(use with caution as may amplify)*, Crackled Fire Agate, Fire Agate, Galena *(caution toxic)*, Limonite, Master Shamanite, Mohawkite, Nunderite, Nuummite, Purpurite, Richterite, Rose Quartz, Tantalite, Tugtupite. *Chakra:* throat

Ill-wishing, return to source so that effect is understood: Beryl, Bronzite, Calcite, Chalcedony, Quartz, Selenite, Silver. *Chakra:* higher heart

Illusions, dispel: Labradorite, Moonstone, Purple Tourmaline

Inferiority complex: Pyrite in Magnesite, Rhodolite Garnet. *Chakra:* dantien

Inner critic: Charoite and *see Obsessive thoughts*

Inner peace: Amethyst, Ammonite, Blue Lace Agate, Calcite, Chrysoprase, Eye of the Storm (Judy's Jasper), Grape Chalcedony, Jade, Prairie Tanzanite, Rose Quartz, Uvarovite Garnet

Interviews: Citrine, Garnet, Malachite, Sodalite, Sunset Sodalite

Investing without undue risk: Goldstone, Malachite, Peridot, Prehnite

– J –

Jealousy: Eclipse Stone, Heulandite, Rainbow Mayanite, Rosophia, Tugtupite, Zircon. *Chakra:* heart

Joy bringers: Cavansite, Chrysoprase, Citrine, Emerald, Green Tourmaline, Iolite and Sunstone, Mangano Calcite, Orange or Yellow Jade, Pink Chalcedony, Poppy Jasper, Red Calcite, Ruby in Kyanite or Zoisite, Sapphire, Stellar Beam Calcite, Sunstone, Topaz, Yellow or Orange or Golden Calcite

Judgementalism: Blue Lace Agate, Green Heulandite, Mohawkite, Morganite, Rose Quartz, Tantalite. *Chakra:* dantien

– K –

Karma of grace: Amethyst Aura Quartz, Angel Aura Quartz, Celestial Quartz, Chinese Red Quartz, Grape Chalcedony, Himalayan Quartz, Indicolite Quartz, Lapis Lace, Lepidolite, Morganite, Prairie Tanzanite, Temple Calcite

Karpman Triangle: Charoite, Chrome Dioptase, Green Zoisite, Morganite, Moss Agate, Rhodochrosite, Ruby in Zoisite or Kyanite, Sugilite, Thulite (Pink Zoisite), Tourmaline. *Chakra:* heart seed, base, sacral, heart, throat

Knee chakras: Aragonite, Azurite, Blue Lace Agate, Boji Stone, Cathedral Quartz, Chrysanthemum Stone, Dinosaur Bone, Flint, Hematite, Magnetite, Merlinite, Peanut Wood, Petrified Wood, Preseli Bluestone, Shungite with Selenite, Sodalite, Spider Web Obsidian, Stromatolite. *Chakra:* knees

> **balance and align:** Aragonite, Magnetite, Mohawkite, Polychrome Jasper, Preseli Bluestone with chalk
> **spin too rapid/stuck open:** Flint, Hematite, Mohawkite, Polychrome Jasper, Smoky Quartz
> **spin too sluggish/stuck closed:** Fire Opal, Harlequin Quartz, Hematite Quartz

Lack, overcome: Aventurine, Citrine, Eye of the Storm, Rose Quartz. *Chakra:* base, sacral, solar plexus, *and see Abundance*

Lateral thinking: Dumortierite, Fluorite, Green Tourmaline, Jade, Topaz

Letting go of past: Axinite, Fenster Quartz, Fulgarite, Green Diopside, Kakortokite, Kimberlite, Lepidocrocite, Nuummite, Paraiba Tourmaline, Pumice, Scheelite, Zircon. *Chakra:* solar plexus, heart, past life

Life purpose: Long flat Quartz with one absolutely smooth side. Brandenberg Amethyst, Cradle of Life (Humankind), Herkimer Diamond, Lapis Lazuli, Moldavite, Trigonic Quartz, *and see Soulplan*

Light-bringer: Anandalite, Calcite, Quartz, Selenite. *Chakra:* crown, soul star, stellar gateway. Place above head or at top or centre of grid.

Limiting patterns of behaviour: Ajoite, Amphibole, Arfvedsonite, Atlantasite, Barite, Botswana Agate, Bronzite, Cassiterite, Celadonite, Chlorite Shaman Quartz, Crackled Fire Agate, Dalmatian Stone, Datolite, Dream Quartz, Dumortierite, Epidote, Garnet in Quartz, Glendonite, Halite, Hanksite, Hematoid Calcite, Honey Phantom Calcite, Indicolite Quartz, Kinoite, Marcasite, Merlinite, Nuummite, Oligocrase, Owyhee Blue Opal, Pearl Spa Dolomite, Porphyrite (Chinese Letter Stone), Quantum Quattro, Rainbow Covellite, Scheelite, Spider Web Obsidian, Stellar Beam Calcite. *Chakra:* base, sacral, dantien, solar plexus, past life

Luck: Agatised Coral (Star Stone), Aventurine, Jade, Ruby, Tourmaline. *Chakra:* Base

Managing your money: Bloodstone, Chrysanthemum Stone, Cinnabar *(caution toxic)*, Citrine, Garnet, Goldstone, Green Spinel, Jet, Malachite, Prasiolite, Pyrite

Manifestation: Calcite, Celadonite, Chlorite Quartz, Eye of the Storm, Goldstone, Grape Chalcedony, Jade, Malachite, Manifestation Quartz, Obsidian, Rose Quartz, Selenite, Smoky Quartz. *Chakra:* solar plexus, heart, Gaia gateway

Manipulation, block: Black Tourmaline, Mohawkite, Nuummite, Tantalite

Material success: Carnelian, Cinnabar *(caution toxic)*, Citrine, Jet, Manifestation Quartz, Morganite, Quartz Generator, Spinel, square-cut Garnets, Tree Agate

Matriarchy/mother issues: Ancestralite, Gaia's Blood (Red) Flint, Jade, Jasper, Menalite, Moonstone, Shiva Lingam, Spirit Quartz. *Chakra:* navel (tummy button), *and see Parents*

Mental abuse: Apricot Quartz, Lazurine, Proustite, Tugtupite with Nuummite, Yellow Crackle Quartz, Xenotine

Mental agitation: Amethyst, Strawberry Quartz, Youngite

Mental attachments: Aegerine, Banded Agate, Blue Halite, Botswana Agate, Lemurian Seed, Limonite, Pyrolusite, Smoky Amethyst, Yellow Phantom Quartz. *Chakra:* third eye

Mental blockages: Auralite 23, Fluorite, Molybdenite,

Rhodozite

Mental breakdown: Molybdenite, Novaculite, Quantum Quattro, Youngite. *Chakra:* third eye, crown

Mental clarity: Holly Agate, Merkabite Calcite, Moldau Quartz, Poldervaarite, Realgar and Orpiment, Sacred Scribe, Star Hollandite, Thompsonite

Mental cleansing: Black Kyanite, Blue Quartz, Fluorite, Hungarian Quartz

Mental conditioning, rigid: Drusy Golden Healer, Pholocomite, Rainbow Covellite, *and see Outworn patterns page 258. Chakra:* third eye, crown

Mental confusion: Aegerine, Blue Halite, Blue Quartz, Hematoid Calcite, Limonite, Pholocomite, Poldervaarite, Richterite

Mental detox: Amechlorite, Banded Agate, Drusy Quartz on Sphalerite, Eye of the Storm, Larvikite, Pyrite in Magnesite, Rainbow Covellite, Richterite, Shungite, Smoky Quartz with Aegerine, Spirit Quartz, Tantalite

Mental dexterity/flexibility, improve: Brucite, Bushman Quartz, Coprolite, Green Ridge Quartz, Kimberlite, Limonite, Molybdenite, Seriphos Quartz, Tiffany Stone, Titanite (Sphene). *Chakra:* third eye, crown

Mental dysfunction: Alunite, Star Hollandite, Titanite (Sphene)

Mental exhaustion: Cinnabar in Jasper *(caution toxic)*, Marcasite, Spectrolite

Mental focus: Fluorite, Sacred Scribe (Russian Lemurian)

Mental imperatives, release: Golden Danburite, Nuummite, Septarian, Tantalite. *Chakra:* past life

Mental implants: Amechlorite, Blue Halite, Brandenberg, Cryolite, Drusy Golden Healer, Holly Agate, Ilmenite, Lemurian Aquitane Calcite, Novaculite, Nuummite, Pholocomite, Tantalite

Mental sabotage: Agrellite, Amphibole, Lemurian Aquitane Calcite, Mohawkite, Paraiba Tourmaline, Tantalite, Yellow Scapolite

Mental strength: Plancheite

Mental, undue influence, remove: Limonite, Novaculite, Tantalite

Mental upheaval: Guinea Fowl Jasper

Mind, butterfly: Amazez, Auralite 23, Fluorite, Tantalite

Miser: Peridot, Pyrite

Mistrust: Amethyst, Anandalite, Grape Chalcedony, Prairie Tanzanite, Rosophia, Topaz, Turquoise. *Chakra:* heart

Motivation: Carnelian, Citrine, Red Jasper, Triplite

– N –

Negative self-image: Carnelian, Citrine, Golden Calcite, Lepidolite, Rose Quartz, Sodalite. *Chakra:* heart

Neurotic patterns: Arfvedsonite, Celadonite, Greenlandite, Porphyrite (Chinese Letter Stone), Rainbow Covellite, Scheelite. *Chakra:* solar plexus

New beginnings: Amazonite, Aragonite, Celestite, Citrine, Emerald, Garnet, Green Tourmaline, Iron Pyrite, Kyanite, Labradorite, Lemon Chrysoprase, Mookaite Jasper, Moonstone, Moss Agate, Rhodonite, Rose Quartz, Sunstone, Tanzurine, Tiger's Eye, Turquoise, White Calcite. *Timing: new moon.*

New business: Bumble Bee Jasper *(caution toxic)*, Citrine, Dalmatian Stone, Goldstone, Mookaite Jasper, Peach Moonstone, Petrified Wood, Sodalite, Sunstone. *Grid around new premises.*

Nurturing, lack of: Amblygonite, Bornite on Silver, Calcite Fairy Stone, Clevelandite, Cobalto Calcite, Drusy Blue Quartz, Flint, Jade, Jasper, Lazurine, Menalite, Mount Shasta Opal, Ocean Jasper, Prasiolite, Rose Quartz, Ruby Lavender Quartz, Septarian, Super 7, Tree Agate, Tugtupite. *Chakra:* higher heart, base

Obsessive thoughts: Ammolite, Auralite 23, Barite, Bytownite, Fluorite, Scolecite, Spirit Quartz, Tantalite. *Chakra:* third eye, crown

Old story retelling: Lapis Lace, Peridot, Scheelite

Optimism: Carnelian, Citrine, Red Jasper, Topaz

Other people's thoughts invading: Amethyst, Auralite 23, Black Tourmaline, Fluorite, Labradorite, Shamanite. *Chakra:* third eye

Outworn patterns: Amphibole, Arfvedsonite, Brandenberg Amethyst, Celadonite, Garnet in Quartz, Owyhee Blue Opal, Porphyrite (Chinese Letter Stone), Quantum Quattro, Rainbow Covellite, Rainbow Mayanite, Scheelite, Stibnite *(caution toxic)*. *Chakra:* earth star, base, sacral, solar plexus, third eye

Over-attachment: Drusy Golden Healer, Rainbow Mayanite, Tantalite, Tinguaite. *Chakra:* solar plexus, navel (tummy button)

Overspending: Amber, Amethyst, Malachite, Peridot

Over-thinking: Amazez, Auralite 23, Bytownite, Creedite, Dalmatian Stone, Rhomboid Selenite. *Chakra:* third eye

– P –

Painful feelings, assimilate: Blue Lace Agate, Khutnohorite, Mangano Calcite, Pinolith, Rhodolite Garnet, Tugtupite. *Chakra:* heart

Palm chakras: Flint, Quartz, Spangolite
  balance and align: Anandalite, Quartz
  spin too rapid/stuck open: Flint, Granite, Hematite
  spin too sluggish/stuck open: Quartz, Spangolite
  Note: Any crystal will open the palm chakras.

Parents: Ancestralite, Onyx, Shiva Lingam. *Chakra:* dantien, navel (tummy button), base and sacral
  father: Citrine, Green Tourmaline, Jasper, Mentor formation, Milky Way (Blue-white) Flint, Pietersite, Sunstone
  integrate the inner parents: Gaia's Blood and Milky Way Flint, Day and Night Quartz, Shiva Lingam
  mother: Gaia's Blood (Red) Flint, Larimar, Menalite, Moonstone, Mother and child formation, Picture Jasper, Rhodochrosite, Rose Quartz, Selenite

And see Matriarchy/mother issues and Patriarchy/father issues.

Past life chakras: Ammolite, Astraline, Black Moonstone, Blizzard Stone, Brandenberg Amethyst, Catlinite, Chrysotile, Chrysotile in Serpentine, Coprolite, Cuprite with Chrysocolla, Dinosaur Bone, Dumortierite, Ethiopian Opal, Fire and Ice, Flint, Keyiapo, Larvikite, Lemurian Aquitane Calcite, Madagascar Quartz, Mystic Merlinite, Oceanite (Blue Onyx), Peanut Wood, Petrified

Wood, Preseli Bluestone, Rainbow Mayanite, Rainbow Moonstone, Reinerite, Rhodozite, Rhyolite, Scheelite, Serpentine in Obsidian, Shiva Lingam, Smoky Amethyst, Tangerose, Tantalite, Titanite, Variscite, Violane (Blue Dioptase), Voegesite, Wind Fossil Agate

> **balance and align:** Dumortierite, Picasso Jasper, Rainbow Mayanite, Tangerose, Titanite, Violane (Blue Dioptase)
>
> **spin too rapid/stuck open:** Black Moonstone, Coprolite, Flint, Petrified Wood, Preseli Bluestone, Scheelite, Sea Sediment Jasper, Tantalite
>
> **spin too sluggish/stuck closed:** Blizzard Stone, Dragon Stone, Dumortierite, Garnet in Quartz, Rhodozite, Serpentine in Obsidian, Tantalite

Patriarchy/father issues: Ancestralite, Onyx, Sunstone. *Chakra:* base and sacral

People-pleaser, release: Anthrophyllite, Morganite. *Chakra:* dantien

Persistence: Adamite, Agate, Flint, Hematite, Moss Agate, Onyx, Red Chalcedony, self-healed crystals, Snowflake Obsidian

Philanthropy: Topaz

Planning meeting: Brandenberg Amethyst, Stellar Beam Calcite, Trigonic Quartz, *and see Soulplan*

'Poor me' syndrome/victim mentality/Karpman dramas: Chrome Dioptase, Eye of the Storm, Green Zoisite, Kiwi Jasper, Lemurian Jade, Morganite, Rhodochrosite, Rose Quartz, Sugilite, Thulite. *Chakra:* solar plexus and heart

Positivity: Chalcedony, Iron Pyrite, Sunstone

Poverty consciousness: Aventurine, Citrine, Eye of the Storm, Goldstone, Green Calcite, Peridot. *Chakra:* base

Practicality: Agate, Onyx

Problem solving: Amazez, Aventurine, Fluorite, Graphic Smoky Quartz, Topaz

Prosperity: Ammolite, Carnelian, Citrine, Goldstone, Green Aventurine, Jade, Tiger's Eye, Turquoise, Yellow Sapphire

Protection, from crime and/or violence: Jet, Sardonyx, Selenite, Turquoise

Protection, home, other buildings: Black Tourmaline, Dravide Tourmaline, Halite, Hanksite, Holey Stones, Malachite, Quartz, Rose Quartz, Ruby, Sardonyx, Selenite, Witches Finger

Protection, possessions: Ruby, Sardonyx, Zircon

– Q –

Quality of life: *see Joy bringers*

– R –

Realistic goals: Hemimorphite, Purple Tourmaline, Ruby, Tiger's Eye

Reclaim power: Brandenberg Amethyst, Eilat Stone, Empowerite, Leopardskin Jasper, Nuummite, Owyhee Blue Opal, Rainbow Mayanite, Smoky Elestial Quartz, Tinguaite. *Chakra:* past life, base

Reconciliation: Afghanite, Chinese Red Quartz, Pink Lazurine, Rose Quartz, Ruby Lavender Quartz. *Chakra:* heart seed

Regulatory crystals: Aragonite, Black Kyanite, Calcite, Charoite, Chromium Quartz, Fluorite, Green Kyanite, Halite, Isua, Kiwi Stone (Sesame Jasper), Ocean Jasper, Prairie Tanzanite, Quartz, Rose Quartz, Selenite, Serpentine, Shungite, Smoky Quartz, Tanzurine (Cherry and Emerald Quartz)

Releasing vows: Nuummite, Rainbow Mayanite, Stibnite *(caution toxic)*, Wind Fossil Agate. *Chakra:* past life, third eye

Resentment: Eclipse Stone, Eudialyte, Rose Quartz. *Chakra:* base, dantien

Resistance, dissolve: Pink Topaz, Smoky Quartz

Risk taking: Malachite

Sabotage, self: Agrellite, Charoite, Grape Chalcedony, Lapis Lace, Lemurian Aquitane Calcite, Mohawkite, Morganite, Prairie Tanzanite, Quantum Quattro, Scapolite, Scheelite, Turquoise

Sacral chakra: Amber, Amphibole, Bastnasite, Black Opal, Blue Jasper, Blue-green Fluorite, Blue-green Turquoise, Bumble Bee Jasper *(caution toxic)*, Carnelian, Chinese Red Quartz, Citrine, Clinohumite, Golden and iron-coated Green Ridge Quartz, Golden Healer Quartz, Keyiapo, Limonite, Mahogany Obsidian, Orange Calcite, Orange Carnelian, Orange Kyanite, Orange Zincite, Realgar and Orpiment, Red Amethyst, Red Jasper, Red/Orange Zincite, Tangerose, Topaz, Triplite, Vanadinite

>**balance and align:** Anandalite, Celestobarite, Golden Healer Quartz, Green Ridge Quartz

>**spin too rapid/stuck open:** Amber, Black Opal, Blue-green Fluorite, Blue-green Turquoise

>**spin too sluggish/stuck closed:** Carnelian, Orange Zincite, Topaz, Triplite

Saviour/rescuer complex: Cassiterite, Chrome Diopside, Chrysoprase, Fuchsite, Malachite, Morganite, Peridot, Prehnite, Sugilite, Thulite

Scapegoat: Charoite, Eye of the Storm, Morganite, Scapolite

Scapegoating behaviour: Champagne Aura Quartz, Mohawkite, Scapolite, Smoky Amethyst

Security issues: Chinese Red Quartz, Eye of the Storm, Nzuri Moyo, Prairie Tanzanite, Red Jasper. *Chakra:* base

Self-acceptance: Lavender Quartz, Lemurian Seed, Mangano Calcite, Orange Phantom, Peach Selenite, Pink Sunstone, Quantum Quattro, Rose Quartz, Tangerose, Tugtupite. *Chakra:* heart, higher heart

Self-confidence: Blue Quartz, Lemurian Seed, Nunderite, Pink Sunstone. *Chakra:* solar plexus

Self-defeating programs, overcome: Desert Rose, Drusy Quartz, Kinoite, Nuummite, Paraiba Tourmaline, Quantum Quattro, Strawberry Quartz

Self-discipline: Blue Quartz, Dumortierite, Scapolite, Sillimanite

Self-esteem: Citrine, Eisenkiesel, Graphic Smoky Quartz (Zebra Stone), Hackmanite, Lazulite, Mangano Calcite, Morion, Nzuri Moyo, Pink Phantom, Strawberry Quartz, Tinguaite. *Chakra:* base, sacral, dantien, heart, higher heart

Self-forgiveness: Chinese Red Quartz, Eudialyte, Mangano Calcite, Pink Crackle Quartz, Rose Quartz, Spirit Quartz, Steatite, Tugtupite. *Chakra:* heart

Self-hatred (combating): Blizzard Stone, Mangano Calcite, Quantum Quattro, Tugtupite. *Chakra:* base

Sensible spending: Green Quartz (Prasiolite), Green Tourmaline, Hematite, Jet and Peridot, *and see Managing your money*

Service: Agatised Coral (Star Stone, Petrosky Stone), Amazez, Amethyst, Dioptase, Indicolite (Blue) Tourmaline, Pink Calcite, Quartz, Selenite. *Chakra:* heart, causal vortex

Shadow, integrate: Amazez, Amethyst Aura Quartz, Iolite and Sunstone, Kammerite, Morion, Obsidian, Proustite, Smoky Lemurian Seed, Smoky Quartz, Voegesite

Slavery, release from: Apache Tear, Freedom Stone, Malachite, Rainbow Obsidian, Rutilated Quartz, Snowflake Obsidian

Solar plexus chakra: Calcite, Citrine, Citrine Herkimer, Golden Azeztulite, Golden Beryl, Golden Calcite, Golden Coracalcite, Golden Danburite, Golden Enhydro, Golden Healer, Golden Labradorite (Bytownite), Green Chrysoprase, Green Prehnite, Green Ridge Quartz, Jasper, Libyan Glass Tektite, Light Green Hiddenite, Malachite, Obsidian, Rainbow Obsidian, Rhodochrosite, Rhodozite, Smoky Quartz, Sunstone, Tangerine Aura Quartz, Tangerine Dream Lemurian Seed, Tiger's Eye, Yellow Tourmaline, Yellow Zincite

> **balance and align:** Anandalite, Citrine, Lemurian Seed

> **spin too rapid/stuck open:** Calcite, Light Green Hiddenite, Malachite, Rainbow Obsidian, Smoky Quartz

> **spin too sluggish/stuck closed:** Golden Calcite, Golden Danburite, Tangerine Aura Quartz, Yellow Labradorite (Bytownite)

Soma chakra: Afghanite, Amechlorite, Angelinite, Angel's Wing Calcite, Astraline, Auralite 23, Azeztulite, Banded Agate, Brandenberg Amethyst, Champagne Aura

Quartz, Crystal Cap Amethyst, Diaspore (Zultanite), Faden Quartz, Fire and Ice, Holly Agate, Ilmenite, Isis Calcite, Lemurian Aquitane Calcite, Merkabite Calcite, Natrolite, Nuummite, Owyhee Blue Opal, Pentagonite, Petalite, Phantom Calcite, Phenacite on Fluorite, Preseli Bluestone, Red Amethyst, Sacred Scribe, Satyaloka and Satyamani Quartz, Scolecite, Sedona Stone, Shaman Quartz, Stellar Beam Calcite, Trigonic Quartz, Violane, Z-stone

> **balance and align:** Bytownite, Diaspore, Stellar Beam Calcite, Violane
>
> **spin too rapid/stuck open:** Isis Calcite, Pinky-beige Ussingite, Sedona Stone, Shaman Quartz, White Banded Agate
>
> **spin too sluggish/stuck closed:** Banded Agate, Diaspore, Nuummite, Preseli Bluestone

Soul agreements, recognition and renegotiation: Ajoite, Amphibole Quartz, Brandenberg Amethyst, Green Ridge Quartz, Indicolite Quartz, Nuummite, Trigonic Quartz, Wind Fossil Agate. *Chakra:* past life, higher crown, *and see Soul contracts*

Soul contracts, clear: Ajoite, Chinese Red Quartz, Chrysotile, Dumortierite, Girasol, Kakortokite, Kyanite, Lemurian Jade, Leopardskin Jasper, Leopardskin Serpentine, Lepidocrocite, Paraiba Tourmaline, Pietersite, Pyrophyllite, Rooster Booster, Trigonic, Wind Fossil Agate

Soul imperatives, clear: Anandalite, Brandenberg, Celestial Quartz, Ice Quartz, Temple Calcite, Trigonic

Quartz

Soul star chakra: Afghanite, Ajoite, Amethyst Elestial, Amphibole, Anandalite, Angel's Wing Calcite, Apophyllite, Astraline, Auralite 23, Azeztulite, Blue Flint, Brandenberg Amethyst, Celestite, Celestobarite, Chevron Amethyst, Citrine, Danburite, Dianite, Diaspore (Zultanite), Elestial Quartz, Fire and Ice, Fire and Ice and Nirvana Quartz, Golden Enhydro Herkimer, Golden Himalayan Azeztulite, Green Ridge Quartz, Hematite, Herkimer Diamond, Holly Agate, Keyiapo, Khutnohorite, Kunzite, Lapis Lazuli, Lavender Quartz, Merkabite Calcite, Muscovite, Natrolite, Novaculite, Nuummite, Onyx, Orange River Quartz, Petalite, Phenacite, Phenacite in Feldspar, Prophecy Stone, Purple Siberian Quartz, Purpurite, Quartz, Rainbow Mayanite, Rosophia, Satyamani and Satyaloka Quartz, Scolecite, Selenite, Shungite, Snowflake Obsidian, Spirit Quartz, Stellar Beam Calcite, Sugilite, Tangerine Aura Quartz, Tanzanite, Tanzine Aura Quartz, Titanite (Sphene), Trigonic Quartz, Vera Cruz Amethyst, Violane, White Elestial

balance and align: Anandalite, Vera Cruz Amethyst, Violane

spin too rapid/stuck open: Celestobarite, Novaculite, Nuummite, Pinky-beige Ussingite, White, Rose or Smoky Elestial Quartz

spin too sluggish/stuck closed: Golden Himalayan Azeztulite, Petalite, Phenacite, Rosophia

Soulplan: Ammolite, Astrophyllite, Blue Aragonite,

Brandenberg Amethyst, Brazilianite, Cacoxenite, Candle Quartz, Cathedral Quartz, Datolite, Dogtooth Calcite, Dumortierite, Elestial Quartz, Fulgarite, Geothite, Golden Danburite, Hackmanite, Hemimorphite, Icicle Calcite, 'key' or 'record keeper' formation, Kyanite, Lemurian Seed, Mystic Topaz, Neptunite, Orange River Quartz, Record Keeper Ruby, Shiva Shell, Spirit Quartz, Star Stone, Stellar Beam Calcite, Trigonic Quartz. *Chakra:* third eye, past life, soma, causal vortex

Speak out: Blue Lace Agate, Honey Opal, Lapis Lace, Titanite (Sphene), Xenotine. *Chakra:* throat

Spirituality: *see soma, third eye and soul star crystals*

Spleen chakra: Amber, Aventurine, Bloodstone, Carnelian, Charoite, Chlorite Quartz, Emerald, Eye of the Storm, Fire Opal, Flint, Gaspeite, Green Fluorite, Jade, Orange River Quartz, Prasiolite, Rhodochrosite, Rhodonite, Ruby, Tugtupite, Zircon

    balance and align: Charoite, Emerald, Eye of the Storm, Flint, Green Aventurine, Tugtupite

    clear attachments and hooks: Aventurine, Chert, Flint, Gaspeite, Jade, Jasper, Lemurian Seed

    for the right armpit: Bloodstone, Eye of the Storm, Gaspeite, Triplite, Tugtupite

    spin too rapid/stuck open: Amber, Aventurine, Chlorite Quartz, Eye of the Storm, Flint, Gaspeite, Green Fluorite, Jade, Prasiolite, Tugtupite

    spin too sluggish/stuck closed: Fire Opal, Orange River Quartz, Rhodonite, Ruby, Topaz

Stellar gateway chakra: Afghanite, Ajoite, Amethyst

Elestial, Amphibole, Anandalite™, Angelinite, Angel's Wing Calcite, Apophyllite, Astraline, Azeztulite, Brandenberg Amethyst, Celestite, Dianite, Diaspore (Zultanite), Elestial Quartz, Fire and Ice, Golden Himalayan Azeztulite, Golden Selenite, Green Ridge Quartz, Holly Agate, Ice Quartz, Kunzite, Merkabite Calcite, Moldavite, Nirvana Quartz, Novaculite, Petalite, Phenacite, Purpurite, Stellar Beam Calcite, Titanite (Sphene), Trigonic Quartz, White Elestial Quartz

> **balance and align:** Ajoite, Amethyst Elestial, Anandalite, Brandenberg Amethyst, Kunzite
>
> **spin too rapid/stuck open:** Amphibole Quartz, Ice Quartz, Merkabite Calcite, Pinky-beige Ussingite, Purpurite
>
> **spin too sluggish/stuck closed:** Angel's Wing Calcite, Diaspore, Phenacite

Study support: Amethyst, Ammolite, Fluorite, Jade, Pyrite, Sodalite, Sugilite

Subconscious blocks: Lepidocrocite, Molybdenite in Quartz, Smoky Elestial Quartz, Smoky Spirit Quartz. *Chakra:* dantien, soul star, stellar gateway, causal vortex, third eye, soma

Succeeding in your goals: Citrine, Hemimorphite, Manifestation Quartz, Quartz Generator, Red Chalcedony, Ruby, Tiger's Eye, Topaz, Turquoise

Sudden energy drain: Agate, Apache Tear, Black Tourmaline, Carnelian, Green Aventurine, Green Fluorite, Jade, Labradorite, Polychrome Jasper, Red Jasper, Shungite, Triplite

Survival instinct: Ammolite, Dragon Stone, Garnet, Kambaba Jasper, Petrified Wood, Stromatolite

Survivor guilt: Anandalite, Chrysocolla, Cradle of Life (Humanity), Flint, Freedom Stone, Isua, Jade, Nuummite, Rose Quartz, Selenite. *Chakra:* heart and solar plexus

Team spirit: Candle Quartz, Grape Chalcedony, Scolecite, Spirit Quartz

Third eye (brow) chakra: Afghanite, Ajo Quartz, Ajoite, Amber, Amechlorite, Amethyst, Ammolite, Amphibole Quartz, Angelite, Apophyllite, Aquamarine, Axinite, Azurite, Black Moonstone, Blue Calcite, Blue Kyanite, Blue Lace Agate, Blue Obsidian, Blue Selenite, Blue Topaz, Blue Tourmaline, Bytownite (Yellow Labradorite), Cacoxenite, Cavansite, Champagne Aura Quartz, Diaspore, Electric-blue Obsidian, Eye of the Storm, Garnet, Glaucophane, Golden Himalayan Azeztulite, Herderite, Herkimer Diamond, Holly Agate, Howlite, Indigo Auram, Iolite, Kunzite, Labradorite, Lapis Lazuli, Lavender-purple Opal, Lazulite, Lepidolite, Libyan Gold Tektite, Malachite with Azurite *(use as polished stone, create essence by indirect method)*, Moldavite, Pietersite, Purple Fluorite, Rhomboid Selenite, Sapphire, Serpentine in Obsidian, Sodalite, Spectrolite, Stilbite, Sugilite, Tangerine Aura Quartz, Turquoise, Unakite, Yellow Labradorite (Bytownite)

   balance and align: Anandalite, Sugilite

   spin too rapid/stuck open: Diaspore, Iolite, Lavender-purple Opal, Pietersite, Serpentine in Obsidian, Sodalite, Sugilite

   spin too sluggish/stuck closed: Apophyllite, Azurite, Banded Agate, Diaspore, Herkimer Diamond, Optical Calcite, Rhomboid Calcite, Rhomboid Selenite, Royal

Blue Sapphire, Tanzine Aura Quartz, Yellow Labradorite (Bytownite)

Thought form, disperse: Aegerine, Firework Obsidian, Fluorite, Nuummite, Rainbow Mayanite, Scolecite, Smoky Amethyst, Smoky Citrine, Spectrolite, Stibnite *(caution toxic)*. *Chakra:* third eye, causal vortex

Throat chakra: Ajo Quartz, Ajoite, Amber, Amethyst, Aquamarine, Astraline, Azurite, Blue Chalcedony, Blue Kyanite, Blue Lace Agate, Blue Obsidian, Blue Quartz, Blue Topaz, Blue Tourmaline (Indicolite), Chalcanthite, Chrysocolla, Chrysotile, Eye of the Storm, Glaucophane, Green Ridge Quartz, Indicolite Quartz, Kunzite, Lapis Lace, Lapis Lazuli, Lepidolite, Moldavite, Paraiba Tourmaline, Sugilite, Turquoise

> **balance and align:** Anandalite, Blue Chalcedony, Blue Lace Agate, Blue Topaz, Indicolite Quartz, Sapphire
>
> **spin too rapid/stuck open:** Black Sapphire, Lepidolite, Paraiba Tourmaline, Sugilite, Turquoise
>
> **spin too sluggish/stuck closed:** Chrysocolla, Lapis Lazuli, Moldavite, Turquoise

Time out: Almandine Garnet, Andradite Garnet, Eye of the Storm, Labradorite, Lapis Lace, Prairie Tanzanite

Toxic thoughts and emotions: Black Amber, Emerald, Fluorite, Sacred Scribe, Selenite, Smoky Quartz, *and see thoughts and emotions*

True Self: Brandenberg Amethyst, Iolite and Sunstone, Trigonic Quartz

Trust: Calcite, Grape Chalcedony, Iron Pyrite, Kunzite, Lavender Jade, Peridot, Prehnite, Rose Quartz, Rubellite

(Pink Tourmaline), Temple Calcite
Truth: Amazonite, Amethyst Aura Quartz, Aqua Aura Quartz, Azurite, Blue Lace Agate, Celestite, Chalcedony Tears, Green Kyanite, Lapis Lazuli

– U –

Undermined: *see Sabotage and Scapegoat*

– V –

Vampirism of heart energy: Amazez, Aventurine, Gaspeite, Greenlandite, Iridescent Pyrite, Lemurian Aquitane Calcite, Nunderite, Tantalite, Xenotine. *Chakra:* solar plexus, heart, higher heart

Vampirism of spleen energy: Gaspeite, Iridescent Pyrite, Nunderite, Tantalite, Xenotine. *Chakra:* spleen

Vibrational change, facilitate: Anandalite, Bismuth, Gabbro, Huebnerite, Lemurian Gold Opal, Lemurian Jade, Lemurian Seed, Luxullianite, Montebrasite, Mtrolite, Nunderite, Orange Natrolite, Orange Sphalerite, Rainbow Mayanite, Rosophia, Sanda Rosa Azeztulite, Snakeskin Pyrite, Sonora Sunrise, Trigonic Quartz. *Chakra:* higher heart, higher crown

Visualisation: Actinolite, Apophyllite, Azurite, Black Moonstone, Iolite and Sunstone, Kyanite, Labradorite, Lapis Lazuli, Moonstone, Preseli Bluestone, Rhomboid Selenite. *Chakra:* third eye, *and see Third eye crystals*

Vows, release: Andean Opal, Dumortierite, Libyan Gold Tektite, Nuummite, Rainbow Mayanite. *Chakra:* past life

– W –

'White Rabbit' syndrome: Eye of the Storm, Grape Chalcedony, Lapis Lace, Prairie Tanzanite, Red or Yellow Calcite

Willpower: Garnet, Hematite, Pyrite, Red Jasper, Rhodonite, Rhyolite, Tiger Iron, Tiger's Eye, Yellow Jasper, Yellow Sapphire

Work-leisure balance: Agate, Almandine Garnet, Andradite Garnet, Aventurine, bicoloured crystals, Calcite, Grape Chalcedony, Lavender Jade, Merlinite, Prairie Tanzanite, Shiva Lingam, Turquoise

Worth, self: Eye of the Storm, *and see Self*

Writing: Calligraphy Stone, Chinese Writing Stone, Graphic Smoky Quartz, Lapis Lazuli, Pink Chalcedony, Triplite

– X, Y, Z –

Zapped: *see Vampirism*
Zealotry: Moonstone

Further Reading and Resources

Judy Hall's Crystal Companion (Hamlyn, London, 2018)
Judy Hall:

The Crystal Bible, Volume 1 (Godsfield Press, London, 2003)
The Crystal Bible, Volume 2 (Godsfield Press, London, 2009)
The Crystal Bible, Volume 3 (Godsfield Press, London, 2013)
Crystal Prescriptions, Volumes 1–7 (O-Books, Alresford, UK)
The Ultimate Guide to Crystal Grids: Transform Your Life Using the Power of Crystals and Layouts paperback (Fair Winds Press, 8 December 2017)
Crystal Mindfulness (Watkins Publishing, London, 2016)
101 Power Crystals (Fair Winds, USA; Quarto, London, 2011)
The Crystal Wisdom Healing Oracle (Watkins Publishing, London, 2016)
The Book of Why (Flying Horse Publications, 2010)

Resources

Petaltone Essences: www.petaltone.co.uk
Judy Hall crystals: www.astrologywise.co.uk
US crystal supplier: www.exquisitecrystals.com

Acknowledgements

Judy Hall would like to acknowledge and thank all the crystal suppliers who have introduced me to some amazing stones, the workshop participants who have helped me to explore their properties and bring abundance into all our lives. Particular thanks to David Eastoe of Petaltone Essences without whose crystal clearing essences I could not work. For further details see www.judyhall.co.uk. I would also like to thank Sue Lilly for drawing my attention to the Karpman Drama Triangle and Brian Parsons for some of the possible solutions.

The Crystal Prescriptions series

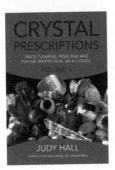

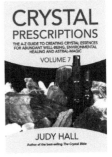

Other Books by Judy Hall

The Alchemy of Night (Roundfire, 2019)

The Magical Sexual Practices of Ancient Egypt
(O-Books, 2019)

Torn Clouds (O-Books, 2004)

SPIRITUALITY

O is a symbol of the world, of oneness and unity; this eye represents knowledge and insight. We publish titles on general spirituality and living a spiritual life. We aim to inform and help you on your own journey in this life. If you have enjoyed this book, why not tell other readers by posting a review on your preferred book site?

Recent bestsellers from O-Books are:

Heart of Tantric Sex

Diana Richardson

Revealing Eastern secrets of deep love and intimacy to Western couples.

Paperback: 978-1-90381-637-0 ebook: 978-1-84694-637-0

Crystal Prescriptions

The A-Z guide to over 1,200 symptoms and their healing crystals

Judy Hall

The first in the popular series of eight books, this handy little guide is packed as tight as a pill-bottle with crystal remedies for ailments.

Paperback: 978-1-90504-740-6 ebook: 978-1-84694-629-5

The 7 Myths about Love...Actually!

The Journey from your HEAD to the HEART of your
SOUL

Mike George

Smashes all the myths about LOVE.

Paperback: 978-1-84694-288-4 ebook: 978-1-84694-682-0

The Holy Spirit's Interpretation of the New Testament

A Course in Understanding and Acceptance

Regina Dawn Akers

Following on from the strength of *A Course In Miracles*,
NTI teaches us how to experience the love and oneness
of God.

Paperback: 978-1-84694-085-9 ebook: 978-1-78099-083-5

The Message of A Course In Miracles

A translation of the Text in plain language

Elizabeth A. Cronkhite

A translation of A Course in Miracles into plain,
everyday language for anyone seeking inner peace. The
companion volume, *Practicing A Course In Miracles*, offers
practical lessons and mentoring.

Paperback: 978-1-84694-319-5 ebook: 978-1-84694-642-4

Thinker's Guide to God

Peter Vardy

An introduction to key issues in the philosophy of
religion.

Paperback: 978-1-90381-622-6

Your Simple Path
Find Happiness in every step
Ian Tucker
A guide to helping us reconnect with what is really
important in our lives.
Paperback: 978-1-78279-349-6 ebook: 978-1-78279-348-9

365 Days of Wisdom
Daily Messages To Inspire You Through The Year
Dadi Janki
Daily messages which cool the mind, warm the heart
and guide you along your journey.
Paperback: 978-1-84694-863-3 ebook: 978-1-84694-864-0

Body of Wisdom
Women's Spiritual Power and How it Serves
Hilary Hart
Bringing together the dreams and experiences of women
across the world with today's most visionary spiritual
teachers.
Paperback: 978-1-78099-696-7 ebook: 978-1-78099-695-0

Dying to Be Free
From Enforced Secrecy to Near Death to True
Transformation
Hannah Robinson
After an unexpected accident and near-death experience,
Hannah Robinson found herself radically transforming
her life, while a remarkable new insight altered her

relationship with her father, a practising Catholic priest.
Paperback: 978-1-78535-254-6 ebook: 978-1-78535-255-3

The Ecology of the Soul

A Manual of Peace, Power and Personal Growth for Real
People in the Real World
Aidan Walker
Balance your own inner Ecology of the Soul to regain
your natural state of peace, power and wellbeing.
Paperback: 978-1-78279-850-7 ebook: 978-1-78279-849-1

Not I, Not other than I

The Life and Teachings of Russel Williams
Steve Taylor, Russel Williams
The miraculous life and inspiring teachings of one of the
World's greatest living Sages.
Paperback: 978-1-78279-729-6 ebook: 978-1-78279-728-9

On the Other Side of Love

A woman's unconventional journey towards wisdom
Muriel Maufroy
When life has lost all meaning, what do you do?
Paperback: 978-1-78535-281-2 ebook: 978-1-78535-282-9

Practicing A Course In Miracles

A translation of the Workbook in plain language, with
mentor's notes
Elizabeth A. Cronkhite
The practical second and third volumes of The Plain-

Language *A Course In Miracles*.
Paperback: 978-1-84694-403-1 ebook: 978-1-78099-072-9

Quantum Bliss

The Quantum Mechanics of Happiness, Abundance, and Health

George S. Mentz

Quantum Bliss is the breakthrough summary of success and spirituality secrets that customers have been waiting for.

Paperback: 978-1-78535-203-4 ebook: 978-1-78535-204-1

The Upside Down Mountain

Mags MacKean

A must-read for anyone weary of chasing success and happiness – one woman's inspirational journey swapping the uphill slog for the downhill slope.

Paperback: 978-1-78535-171-6 ebook: 978-1-78535-172-3

Your Personal Tuning Fork

The Endocrine System

Deborah Bates

Discover your body's health secret, the endocrine system, and 'twang' your way to sustainable health!

Paperback: 978-1-84694-503-8 ebook: 978-1-78099-697-4

Readers of ebooks can buy or view any of these bestsellers by clicking on the live link in the title. Most titles are published in paperback and as an ebook. Paperbacks are available in traditional bookshops. Both print and ebook formats are available online.

Find more titles and sign up to our readers' newsletter at http://www.johnhuntpublishing.com/mind-body-spirit

Follow us on Facebook at
https://www.facebook.com/OBooks/
and Twitter at https://twitter.com/obooks